Repair &

Reattachment

Grief Therapy

Rochelle Wright, M.S.

R. Craig Hogan, Ph.D.

Contact:

Greater Reality Publications
http://greaterreality.com
800 827-3770
Email: info@greaterreality.com
Order copies: http://orders.greaterreality.com

ISBN 9781519661678

Acknowledgments

To all of the wonderful clients and experiencers I have had the pleasure of working with on the very sacred material of their lives.

To my friends and fellow therapists who listened and encouraged me when I was excited, happy, surprised and overwhelmed as the birth of this book unfolded.

To my adult children, Libby and Tane, who listened, without judgment, as I told them about the book I was writing about the other side. They were happy for me and what was evolving. They know me well, but continue to be surprised.

Last, but certainly not least, to Craig Hogan, the co-author of the book, who took my call on Christmas Eve morning, December 24, 2009, and immediately shared the excitement of getting this wonderful material out to the world. He is a marvelous, enthusiastic, helpful, and kind person in my life. He is the grease that made the wheels turn to make this happen. I often refer to him as "my best cheerleader."

Contents

v

Preface

I am Rochelle Wright, a licensed psychotherapist from the state of Washington. I've always cared deeply about my clients, especially those suffering from grief over the death of a loved one. I've done whatever I could to help them manage the pain of their loss, but always wished I could do more. Today, I can.

I designed a psychotherapy method that helps grief-stricken people experience a perceived connection with their deceased loved one. We named the new method Repair & Reattachment Grief Therapy.

It uses bilateral stimulation, a powerful method of changing the person's customary patterns of thinking, feeling, and regarding specific memories so the person experiences the thoughts, feelings, and memories from fresh perspectives, perhaps for the first time since childhood.

Source of the Images and Impressions

The source of the images and impressions clients experience makes no difference. The client experiences a profound, lasting alleviation of grief. Whether the experiences come from an inner reservoir of self-healing resources or some other source makes no difference to the grief therapy. It works.

The Case Studies that Follow

This book presents the actual cases of people whom I have helped experience Repair & Reattachment Grief Therapy. The experiences are uplifting, reassuring, and life changing. We want this wonderful gift to humankind to be available to as many people as possible. If you are a state-licensed psychotherapist wanting to know about being trained to facilitate Repair &

Reattachment Grief Therapy, read the chapter titled "For State-Licensed Psychotherapists" at the end of his book.

Repair & Reattachment Grief Therapy

I discovered how we can help people enter the condition of mind in which they can perceive a connection with their loved ones who have died. It is through Repair & Reattachment Grief Therapy. It results in changed lives. For the clients and for us, it is very exciting and very special.

The reactions of the Repair & Reattachment Grief Therapy experiencers are the clearest evidence of the healing power of this connection. While experiencers begin a Repair & Reattachment Grief Therapy session in sorrow or grief, most end it feeling joy, reassurance, and comfort. The traumatic and tragic images that had plagued them for years or decades diminish or are gone, replaced by positive images. The uplifting messages are filled with wise guidance that changes the experiencers' lives.

In Repair & Reattachment Grief Therapy, the experiencers open their own perceptions of connections with their deceased loved ones. The method itself does not induce connections. The psychotherapist has no influence over the nature or content of the connections. The perceived connections occur naturally and effortlessly, emerging when the experiencers enter a receptive mode, just as sleep follows naturally from relaxing into a comfortable bed. The experiences normally occur in five hours, but may continue for a longer period of time.

The psychotherapist helps the experiencer enter a receptive mode using a technique called bilateral stimulation. In it, the experiencer is gently stimulated on the left and right sides of the body, alternately. These stimulations affect the right and left sides of the brain, causing a reorientation of perceptions. We use two modes of bilateral stimulation: listening to music or sounds that alternate in volume between the left and right ears, and moving the eyes rhythmically left and right while keeping the head steady.

Bilateral stimulation is commonly used today to heal post-traumatic stress disorder and a variety of other psychological conditions that don't respond well to conventional psychotherapy. Over 50,000 or more licensed psychotherapists now use bilateral stimulation with clients in a procedure called eye-movement desensitization and reprocessing (EMDR). The procedure has been recognized as a valid psychotherapy method by the American Psychological Association, the Veterans Administration Hospitals, Israeli National Council for Mental Health, Dutch National Steering Committee on Mental Health Care, International Society for Traumatic Stress, French National Institute of Health and Medical Research, National Institute for Clinical Excellence, United Kingdom Department of Health, and other respected bodies.[1] It has been called the "breakthrough therapy for overcoming anxiety, stress, and trauma."[2]

However, this use of bilateral stimulation is not EMDR. It only uses some eye movements as EMDR does. Somehow, bilateral stimulation also opens the person's mind to perceived connections with deceased loved ones. No one knows why bilateral stimulation heals people's psychological problems or results in perceived communications with the deceased, but both happen consistently; it is highly successful and reliable.

The Repair & Reattachment Grief Therapy Procedure

In preparation for the Repair & Reattachment Grief Therapy, the psychotherapist has the person put on headphones to listen to a recording of barely audible music and sounds alternating in volume between the left and right ears. That stimulation of the right and left hearing centers provides audio bilateral stimulation. Experiencers wear the headset during the entire Repair & Reattachment Grief Therapy session, from the time they enter the office and sit down until the session ends, to maintain the audio bilateral stimulation.

The procedure begins by having the experiencer talk about the deceased loved one for as long as an hour or more. Especially important are the memories, images, and thoughts associated with the person's death. After the experiencer finishes telling the story, the psychotherapist tells the experiencer to focus on the image or thought that causes them the most disturbance or grief. The psychotherapist guides the experiencer through a short series of rhythmic eye-movements left and right to provide the visual bilateral stimulation. The therapist also has the client go inside, called natural flow energy exchange, somewhat like a rhythmic tai chi exchange of energy.

Experiencers then close their eyes, focusing on the distressing memory, image, or thought. They have a mental experience, usually for several minutes, but occasionally for 15 minutes or more, and then open their eyes. The experiencers describe what they experienced to the psychotherapist in a few words. The experience could be anything: a memory, unusual scene, feeling of sadness, sensation of warmth, words heard, bodily sensations, swirls of light, sense of a presence, or any other experience.

In the early sets of eye movements, the images and feelings are associated with the distressing image they are focusing on, memories of the deceased, colors, lights, and swirls, or other impressions that are beginning connections. For some people, the perceived connection happens as soon as the processing begins. For others, it comes later in the session, after the psychotherapist has repeated this procedure several times. However, People do not have to return for a second session. However, they may return to target a dream or other such experience. After the first session, most experiencers have the connection more easily, so in later sessions, which last for only 90 minutes, the connection may begin as early as the first set of eye movements.

After the experiencers describe what they experienced while their eyes were closed, the psychotherapist has them focus on that experience, regardless of what it was, and either has the experiencer close his or her eyes and go back inside or repeats the eye movements. There is no discussion or evaluation of what the experiencer describes. The psychotherapist does not guide the experiencer or suggest any direction for the next experience. The psychotherapist simply accepts whatever the experiencer describes, without comment or judgment.

That process occurs repeatedly for the entire Repair & Reattachment Grief Therapy procedure. During the procedure, most people have a perceived connection with their loved ones. After the connection begins, the successive sets of eye movements maintain the relaxed, receptive state and the connection continues, usually for an hour or more, resuming each time the experiencer closes his or her eyes.

The Connections Reorient the Experiencers' Grief

The perceived connections reduce or virtually eliminate the deep grief in which experiencers are immersed. They reorient the beliefs, images, feelings of guilt and anger, trauma, and perspectives on the loved one's death so they are replaced by reassurance, joy, renewed feelings of love and connection, and peace. The sadness at this separation through death is usually desensitized so the person doesn't remember it in the same way — the sadness dissipates. People don't forget their loved ones, but after the Repair & Reattachment Grief Therapy, they see them in a better light — they see them differently — and most of the time the sadness is gone. Repair & Reattachment Grief Therapy makes the grief more bearable and reduces the feeling of separation.

At the beginning of the sessions, the psychotherapist asks the experiencers to describe their memories of the person's death. The experiencers then rate the level of disturbance on a scale of 0 to 10, with 0 being no disturbance and 10 being strong disturbance. Some experiencers rate their most distressing images and memories as 10 plus or even 10 plus, plus, plus, plus.

Following the perceived connection, experiencers usually rate the most disturbing images as 0 to 3. The reduction in their distress is remarkable, and the levels usually process even lower on their own over the next few days, weeks, or even months. These reductions in the levels of distress remain stable over time.

Life Changes from the Repair & Reattachment Grief Therapy

The result of the procedure is that clients sometimes experience startling perspectives and advice that change the experiencers' understanding of and direction for their lives.

Experiencers often come away resolved to reorient their lives, with self-confidence, hope, and clear goals that they pursue in happiness.

The Procedure and Theory Behind It

If you're interested in knowing more about the procedure and theory behind it before reading the cases, read the final chapters of this book beginning with "Explanation of Bilateral Stimulation."

Otherwise, the first chapter on the next pages explains enough about the procedure for you to understand what is occurring as you read these wonderful, heartfelt cases.

The Accounts of Repair & Reattachment Grief Therapy that Follow

The accounts that follow describe real sessions I've held with people who have had connections with their loved ones upon entering this receptive mode. They have agreed to share their experiences to let others know about the life-changing experiences they have had during Repair & Reattachment Grief Therapy.

The stories the experiencers told me about their loved ones and the accounts of the Repair & Reattachment Grief Therapy had to be limited to the important or relevant statements. The histories normally last an hour or more, and the Repair & Reattachment Grief Therapy usually last another two or three hours or longer. However, the statements in this book are the words the experiencers spoke.

Most names and pictures are of the actual experiencers and their deceased loved ones. Some have been changed at the requests of the experiencers. However, the details in every account are faithful records of what actually happened during the Repair & Reattachment Grief Therapy. The experiencers have all been involved in editing the accounts to ensure they accurately represent their experiences.

Some experiences believe the connections are with the real deceased person, now on the other side and willing and available to communicate. We report their perceptions, but make no judgments about the sources of the experiences.

Jourdan's story that follows includes more detail about the procedure so you can see how it unfolds.

Ion, Jourdan's Love

*"I will be there for you, but only
in a different way."*

– Ion's words to Jourdan during her connection

Jourdan sat stoically in my office telling me the story of the love of her life, Ion, who had died a year before. She didn't cry. She couldn't. A year of tears and grief had frozen the flow of her feelings. "I don't see how I can get over this," she said to me.

"Tell me everything about Ion and his death," I said.

Jourdan began her story. "Ion was a loner, but he was a gentle, caring, quiet, affectionate man. He suffered from post-traumatic stress disorder from his childhood and headaches from a blow to his head he suffered while working construction. He became addicted to illegal drugs he took to reduce the headache pain. Eventually, he was arrested because of his drug use and occasional violent episodes. They put him into prison.

"I was a single mother with four kids, working as a nurse at the prison. I was in charge of Ion's medications, so I spent time with him, listening to him talk about his life, childhood traumas, headaches, and drug use. There were no psychological counselors, so I did what I could to help him, and as he confided in me, we grew closer. I soon fell in love with him.

"Ion was let out on a work release for a job. We kept contact, and after a few months, he moved into my big farm house. Our time together was blissful.

"Early one morning, the police came to my house to tell me that Ion had been in a serious car accident. I rushed to the hospital, where I learned that Ion's skull was crushed and he had many internal injuries. He was in a coma. I knew he was dying.

"I stayed there to be with him, but he was unresponsive. After 19 days, I had to leave for a few hours, and when I returned to the hospital, I learned that Ion had been taken out of intensive care and put into a room by himself. I went to the room and found him alone, dying. I frantically went into the hallway calling the code for a crash cart to try to resuscitate him. None of the staff would help.

"I stayed there alone with Ion, bathed him, and held him. The next day, the doctor said flatly, 'We think he's brain dead. We're taking him off the ventilator.' I was indescribably depressed. I kissed him gently, and they turned off the ventilator. I could hear his heart beating. It got slower and slower. Finally, he was gone.

"After a lot of red tape and confusion, they asked me to make arrangements for the body. I took possession of Ion's body and contacted a funeral home, but they wanted $5,000 for a funeral—money I didn't have—so I bought a $50 burial plot and my sons built a beautiful casket for him. We prepared him for burial ourselves. My immediate family came for the burial and we lowered Ion into the ground.

"Ion loved wildflowers, so we planted wildflowers on the freshly turned ground. We made homemade bouquets and put them on the grave. Ion loved homemade bouquets."

When Jourdan finished telling me the story, she looked at me and said, "I'm so depressed."

Jourdan had talked to me for over an hour about Ion and his death. The account you have just read is a very short summary of all that she related to me.

The Repair & Reattachment Grief Therapy

After a few moments, she felt she was ready to continue, so I began the Repair & Reattachment Grief Therapy procedure.

We reviewed the memories Jourdan had just described to determine which were most disturbing to her. We rated each on a scale of 0 to 10 for disturbance, with 0 being no disturbance and 10 being extreme disturbance. She said the most disturbing memory was when he was in the hospital room and she was trying to revive him with no help from the nursing staff.

From the time she began telling me about Ion, Jourdan wore headphones playing barely audible background music and sounds alternating in volume between the left and right ears for audio bilateral stimulation. Now I would add the visual bilateral stimulation while she focused on the distressing memory. I told Jourdan, "Keep that image and the words that go along with it in mind. You're in the hospital room with Ion and no one will help revive him. Follow my fingers." I had her follow my fingers, sweeping left and right in front of her, to perform the eye movement part of the Repair & Reattachment Grief Therapy procedure.

After a set of eye movements, Jourdan closed her eyes. Twenty seconds later, she opened them and described in a few words what she had experienced: "I see the farm." I told her to focus on that and we did the eye movements again. She closed her eyes and after a few seconds, opened them. She described what she experienced, and we used that for the next focus.

I had told Jourdan before we began not to judge what was coming to her. As she described it, I made no comments about it. We were both allowing whatever came to arise naturally. The Repair & Reattachment Grief Therapy must occur on their own, without judging, prompting, discussion of what comes up, or evaluation. There was no talk of possible meanings, interpretations, or how she was feeling. We just continued the process, allowing the experience to grow and bloom on its own.

After Jourdan opened her eyes one time, she said, "Last week, the horse was hurt, in my barn. There was blood all over the place and I was getting ready to go to work. I said in exasperation, 'Where are you Ion? Why did you leave me?' And then, unexplainably, I suddenly felt calm, and I handled it."

After another set of eye movements, Jourdan opened her eyes and said, "Peace is coming up. Just peace." She gave a long, long sigh and looked at me intently. "I'm confused about life after death. Does it exist?"

Then, after 90 minutes of this continued processing, Jourdan closed her eyes following a set of eye movements and in a few seconds opened them, smiling warmly at me and nodding. "Ion came to me just now. He said to me, 'I'm always here. Be happy. You need to grow, to push yourself. It's easier to stay the same. You need to fly.' Rochelle, I felt my love could fix him. But guess what, he came into my life to fix me, to fix me more."

I said to Jourdan, "Ask him if he was there that day in the barn with the wounded horse when you thought of him and felt calm." I guided her through the eye movements and she closed her eyes. When she opened them, she said, "'Yes,' he said, 'I was there, but you did it all by yourself.'" I guided Jourdan through another set of eye movements. She closed her eyes and after a few seconds opened them. "He said to me, 'I didn't want to be chained in a locked cage. I wanted to be free. I will be there for you, but only in a different way. Fly, Jourdan!'"

After a while, Jourdan sensed that his energy had left for now. The Repair & Reattachment Grief Therapy continue as long as the person on the other side is available to communicate. There is always a natural, unmistakable closing when the loved ones involved in the connection indicate the experience is at an end. The Repair & Reattachment Grief Therapy continues until they close them, even if the connections last for one or two hours.

We ended the session. As she left, Jourdan's face was glowing. She came back to my office a few days later. I asked if she wanted to work on any issues. Jourdan said, "I don't have any issues. I feel great. I have peace around his death." She smiled, "My co-workers say, 'What did you do to make your eyes sparkle? You look happy.'" Her smile broadened. "They want to know who my therapist is because they want to come to you. Rochelle, a gift has been given to me. I sense a falling away of judgment. I have changed deeply from the inside."

Jourdan looked at me intently. "I feel free to live my own life. I don't want anyone telling me what to do. This is my life and I'm going to look forward to my children's leaving. I don't know if I want to keep my house anymore."

We then did some Repair & Reattachment Grief Therapy processing. Ion came again and gave Jourdan a message: "This is your year to take care of yourself." Jourdan told me, "I feel so powerful, and that is unusual for me.

"I still feel really good for the first time in my life. I am not depressed. Half of my adult life, since my 20s, I've been on Zoloft,

Lexapro, Prozac and all the rest, but now the whole depression thing has lifted from me.

"In the past, I've felt so heavy, depressed, and frustrated; that was normal. Now I feel completely different. I know what I want to do. I really do. There is so much on my plate. I want to work on my farm. I know Ion is here. That's given me strength. I have a new life, with new plans. I have felt much joy in my home. Now it is like sacred ground." One of Jourdan's neighbors brought her the following plaque. It's meaningful to her after her experience.

Death is nothing at all....

I have only slipped away into the next room. I am I and you are you. Whatever we were to each other, that we are still. Call me by my old familiar name, speak to me in the easy way which you always used. Put no difference into your tone; wear no forced air of solemnity or sorrow. Laugh as we always laughed at the little jokes we enjoyed together. Play, smile, think of me, pray for me. Let my name be ever the household word that it always was. Let it be spoken without effort, without the ghost of a shadow on it. Life means all that it ever meant. It is the same as it ever was; there is absolutely unbroken continuity. What is death but a negligible accident? Why should I be out of mind because I am out of sight? I am waiting for you, for an interval, somewhere very near, just around the corner. All is well.

Canon Scott Holland (1847-1918)

Follow-Up with Jourdan

Jourdan came back to my office several weeks later. She explained that the day before had been the two-year anniversary of Ion's death. "Before I had the Repair & Reattachment Grief Therapy with you, I was an atheist," she said. "I didn't believe in anything. That's why losing Ion was terrible for me. I never would have dreamed that would change. But it has."

Jourdan was taking a nursing class, and she said that during the class, they had been discussing Lazarus, the man whom Jesus raised from the dead. Jourdan asked her instructor, "Why do you think God would raise Lazarus from the dead and not Ion?" The instructor didn't have an answer.

"Rochelle," Jourdan said to me, "can we ask Ion about that?" "Certainly," I replied. After someone has had a Repair & Reattachment Grief Therapy, it is very easy for them to go back to the connection. We did the normal bilateral stimulation eye-movement process and she closed her eyes. When she opened them, she said, "Ion is here. I asked him why he wasn't saved from dying like Lazarus was. He said, 'I needed to go.' That's what he said in the first session we had: 'I needed to go.'"

I guided her through more eye movements and Jourdan received this message: "Ion said, 'People go when it is their time. They are ready to go when they go. Some people come into our lives and go, and you should be thankful for the wonderful memories that we had.'"

Jourdan then said she was concerned about her family. They were pretty dysfunctional, and one of her siblings suffered from Alzheimer's. Jourdan was the "black sheep" of the family. "I'm going to ask Ion what I should do about my family," she said. I guided her through another set of eye movements and she closed her eyes. When she opened them, she said that Ion told her, "Give to your family from your heart, but don't be attached to the outcome."

After more eye movements, Jourdan reported his saying, "Live in the moment, the 'now.' Be open to what is happening today." Jourdan ended the session by saying, "It's like my brain is being bathed and my understanding is going deeper into my mind. I just feel it."

Life Changes from the Repair & Reattachment Grief Therapy

At the beginning of the session, Jourdan rated some of her memories on the scale of 0 to 10 as being 10s, the most severely disturbing. She also said two of the memories were 50s, and one was 100. After the Repair & Reattachment Grief Therapy, she said, "The Repair & Reattachment Grief Therapy took the pain of it away. When I think of Ion, it doesn't really bother me anymore."

Jourdan's sadness was greatly reduced. Some moments of the separation can still bring up sad thoughts. But connecting with Ion helped Jourdan better cope with her grief, confident that he is still with her.

I see Jourdan occasionally now. She is moving forward with her life and is open to opportunities that come her way. She is progressing well by making new decisions about her life. She's right. She is a changed person. And Ion came to her to help that happen.

Kate, Carole's Daughter

"It was her! I know it was her!"

– Carole, after her connection with Kate

"I talked to Kate all the time about her boyfriend," Carole said to me. "I'd say, 'OK, I know you love him, but if you're still with him when you go to college, you'll need to be in a college near a prison, because that's where he'll be.'"

Carole and her friend, Linda, had come to me because both were grieving for their children who had died. Carole's daughter Kate passed away at 18, two years before the sessions, and Linda's

son Martine, age 19, passed away only eight months before. Linda had her Repair & Reattachment Grief Therapy first. She made some contact with Martine and had some messages from him. Linda had visions of a vibrant universe as Martine was seeing it.

Then Carole came in for her session. I asked Carole to describe what happened when Kate died. She adjusted the earphones and began. "Kate left on a Friday night to go to the New Jersey shore with her boyfriend and his mother. My husband, Stephen, and I walked her to her boyfriend's car with her suitcase. We kissed her goodbye and watched them drive off Kate called Saturday morning to say the shore was really packed, but they were fine. That was the last time I ever spoke to her.

"Monday morning at 4 a.m., the police were knocking on our door. Stephen let them in. One of the police officers looked at me apologetically and said, 'There's been an accident. Your daughter was killed.' I jumped on the back of the couch screaming. It was the worst night of my life.

"As the day wore on, we learned what had happened. Kate and her boyfriend were in the car alone when the car left the road and crashed through a guardrail. Other cars stopped when they saw the accident. A kind stranger went down to the car and was with my daughter when she died."

Carole looked at me with tears flowing down her cheeks. "I wasn't there when she took her last breath. People told me that by the time they got to the car, Kate had died instantly. They said she didn't suffer. God gave me my child's death my way, despite how horrible it was."

The Repair & Reattachment Grief Therapy

When she finished telling me about Kate's death, I began the Repair & Reattachment Grief Therapy procedure. We focused on the thought that gave her the most grief: "I wasn't there when Kate took her last breath." I said, "Keep that image and the words that go along with it in mind." I had Carole follow my fingers, sweeping left and right in front of her. When she closed her eyes, the connection began very quickly. "I see Kate!" she said with her eyes closed. "She's trying to touch me and is smiling at me." Carole was reaching her arms out in front of her, eyes still closed, to touch Kate. "I can see her fingers. I can feel her. She's right there in front of me."

I guided Carole through another set of eye movements and she closed her eyes. "I see steps, then a real long path that curves a little. Kate's on my left side, talking to me. Her hand is in back of me. I don't know where we're going, but we're going down a sidewalk, beside a wall. She's still talking to me. There's a tree on the left side above the wall. Kate doesn't have her glasses on and her hair is down. She's walking with me, like we're just going for a walk."

Carole continued excitedly with her eyes closed, "I can hug her. I can touch her hair. Her head is just under my shoulder. Now I'm hugging Kate and she is hugging me. I can see her dress and touch her arms. We've stopped at a tree. There's ivy growing on it. The wall is perfect. The stones are really even."

I guided Carole through another set of eye movements. When she closed her eyes, she continued: "Now we flashed to the accident scene, at the lake. It's dark there. Trees are all along the lake. I can see all the trees. The rain is crashing on the ground where we are. It's loud. Rain is on an angle. I can see the guardrail. Kate is showing it to me. She's above the street not far from the ground. The road is empty. Kate's right in front of me, face forward, looking right at me. I can't see her feet. She's showing me her hands. I can see her fingers and hold them. Her right arm is lying on my hand. Kate's holding it up for me."

After another set of eye movements, Carole closed her eyes again. "Now I see Martine, Linda's son. He passed away eight months ago. He's sitting on his couch looking at me, with one leg up and his arms dangling in a funny pose, smiling. But I can still see Kate. Martine's flashing in and out. Now there are two things going on. Kate's outside and Martine's inside. He has his leg up with his arms in that funny position. I can see Kate's dress, but not the bottom. It keeps going to Martine sitting on the couch being silly. I don't understand this."

Martine

I guided her through another set of eye movements and Carole closed her eyes. "I can see Kate in shorts with flip-flops now. She's crossing the street and I'm looking at her back. Her head is turned looking at me. There's distance between us. I want her to keep walking. I want her to keep going. I will be fine. 'Keep going Kate, keep going,'" Carole said, calling to her daughter in a raised voice. Her eyes were still closed.

"Kate just put her head down a little bit. But she's going. I want her to. She's walking down the path. It's so funny. She wouldn't walk anywhere in this life. Things are different for her on the other side."

After she watched Kate leave, Carole opened her eyes and the Repair & Reattachment Grief Therapy session was over. She laughed and leaned back in her chair. "That was her," she said. "I know it was her." She laughed some more, rolling from side to side in her chair.

"She was barely touching the ground. IT WAS HER! I KNOW IT WAS HER!"

Follow-Up with Carole

After the session, Carole wrote me an email describing a remarkable validation of her connection. She wrote that as she and Linda, Martine's mother, were riding home, she told Linda that she had seen Martine in her Repair & Reattachment Grief Therapy. Carole showed Linda the comical pose he was in, with his leg up and arms dangling. Linda's eyes opened wide. She said when Martine was clowning around, he would make what they called his "monkey pose" with his leg up and arms dangling. It was exactly what Carole saw, without knowing that Martine did that.

The pose was a distinctive message from Martine to let his mom, Linda, know that he was fine, happy, and clowning as he always did.

Life Changes from the Repair & Reattachment Grief Therapy

When Carole began the session, she said that the images and thoughts connected with Kate's death were very distressing, especially the thought that she wasn't there when Kate took her last breath. At the end of the session, Carole was laughing and ecstatic about reconnecting with her daughter, Kate.

Don, Judy's Dad

"Dad's teaching me right now about what I am doing as an adult."

– Judy, on her connection with her father

Judy had heard about Repair & Reattachment Grief Therapy
and wanted to connect with her father, Gerald, who had died five
years earlier. "Dad was an in-charge person," she said. "He
taught himself electronics, and served in the Navy as a certified
radio technician. After he was
discharged, he taught for 36
years in the same school
district. Every night after
dinner, without fail, he would
work two hours on papers for
his students.

"The best memories were
when he was doing something
that he loved to do. He built three homes that we lived in. We
would never have had the homes if my father hadn't built them.
For the first house he built, he studied a book, and from studying
the book, he built the entire house. It was really a challenge.

"I liked to watch him do his carpentry work. He would let me
reach up and hold things for him. Most of the time when I would
reach up to hold something, I had to reach too high for a long
time, so my arms ached, but I loved feeling that we were doing
something important together.

"My father did have a dark side. He was not a
communicator. He would make pronouncements. He decided if
the conversation was over, and if it was over it WAS over. Too
much noise and he would shut it down with some sharp words. I
sensed my mother was afraid of him. He could bring her to tears
just like that. I didn't like that.

"I stayed out of his way. Dad didn't value girls like he did
boys, so he did more with my brothers. I played the first violin in
the orchestra and sang in the chorus. I was in the honor society
and was a tennis champion, but Dad never said anything about
my achievements.

"My father retired at 63 years, and in his early 80s, you could
see him going downhill. It was as though he was growing

backwards. He grew young, like the boy in the Brad Pitt movie, *The Curious Case of Benjamin Button*, until finally he was a toddler. This progression was a terrible strain on my mother.

"He didn't know who I was the last time I visited him. He would say to my mother, 'Charlotte, who's staying in there? Who's staying in that bedroom? Did we have children? How many did we have? What are their names?'

"We bought a TV. We set it up and Dad couldn't even understand how to turn it on and off. He'd go over and push the buttons like a toddler, so Mom had to put tape over them. Finally, he was too much for Mom to take care of, and we looked for homes. We did find one, and I told her, 'You'll know when it's time.'

"Finally, after Dad turned 85, it was time. Mom said to him one day, 'Gerry, we're going for a drive,' as though speaking to a little child. Dad picked up his little bag of shaving items, and Mom and a neighbor lady took him to a care-home. He didn't know what was going on when she left him there with his little bag in his hands. We abandoned Dad. For a long time after that, he stood at the door to his room saying to the staff, 'Charlotte is coming.'

"The day after we left him there, my brother rode his bicycle a long way over to the care-home to see my dad. When Dad opened the door, he looked at my brother blankly. Dad didn't have a clue who he was. It was devastating for my brother, to ride his bicycle all the way over there to see my dad, and then to find him like that.

"My father was just a shell of whom he had been. It was awful. Here was a man who had cared for all of us, had gone to work every day, tended a garden, was a responsible parent, and now he was like an infant, totally cared for, with no dignity left.

"Two days later, Mother collapsed. They took her to the emergency room. We thought she was having a heart attack, but it was just the stress. The doctors said she couldn't visit Dad for a month, so Dad was alone. Charlotte never came. But Mom called every day to get a report.

"Finally, Dad fell at the care-home and broke his hip. His doctor, who had been Mom and Dad's doctor for 20 years, said to me, 'Your dad was a wonderful person, but no home will care for him with a broken hip. He has to have surgery.' So at 85 years old, my father had major surgery on his hip. He died three days later.

"I thought of it as a blessing."

The Repair & Reattachment Grief Therapy

When Judy finished, we paused for a while, then began the Repair & Reattachment Grief Therapy processing. We agreed that the saddest memory for her was when she took her father to the care-home and he just had his little case of shaving things. They had left him and gone back home. "We abandoned him," Judy said. I asked her, "On a scale of 0 to 10, with 10 being the most sad, distressing, and activated, and 0 being none or neutral, how would you rate this memory?" She said it was an 8.5.

I guided her through sets of the eye movements. Each time, Judy would close her eyes, then open them and report what she experienced. Over repeated periods of the procedure, she saw memories of her mother working in the kitchen while her father was in the living room unaware of what was going on. Then Judy saw a series of images of the periods just before and just after her father's death.

Finally, after a few more sets of the eye movements, the connection began. Judy opened her eyes and said, "Dad told me he has been set free. He's not a prisoner of his body anymore. And then I got the message from him, 'Rest, Judy, rest.'"

Soon after that, we stopped for the day. "Rochelle, I'm glad I did this," Judy said. "I feel more connected to my father." I had Judy bring up the memory of leaving her father alone at the care-home that she rated an 8.5 at the beginning of the session. She said it now was a 0.

Five days later, Judy came in for the second session. I asked her, "How are you doing?"

She said, "I'm doing well. I'm doing really well. I had a dream about my father. I've never dreamt about him before."

Judy put on the audio bilateral headphones and relaxed for the Repair & Reattachment Grief Therapy procedure. I said, "Bring up the dream" and guided her through the eye movements. Judy closed her eyes, focusing on the dream about her father.

When she opened her eyes, she said, "He is teaching me. I saw Dad and me in the woods. I remember he used to take me into nature and show me things. He would teach me about flowers and trees and insects. Just now when my eyes were closed, I watched myself as a little girl with my father. He was talking and explaining things."

After more eye movements, Judy opened her eyes with an amazed look on her face: "My father is teaching me, a little girl, about nature, but I got the message that he's also teaching me right now about what I am doing as a woman. That's what the dream was all about. I was the learner as a little girl and I am the learner now. But the other thing is, I'm also the adult woman teaching my little girl self.

"Rochelle, both teaching and learning are gifts I received from my father. He's telling me, 'Be with it rather than think about it. Let the learning be rather than trying to manipulate it.'"

I guided her through another set of eye movements and Judy closed her eyes. When she opened them, she said, "I saw myself as a little girl and as the woman I am now, standing face-to-face. As a little girl, I didn't get the attachment I wanted from my father, and today as a woman, my expectations for attachments are really high. I push my feelings down because I want connections with others so strongly that I don't want to be disappointed."

After another set of eye movements, the connection continued. "I feel as though I'm learning lessons. I got the message that I'm

pushing my feelings down because I am afraid that if I allow
myself to become emotionally open and attached, I will only set
myself up to be disappointed later. They're my feelings coming
from my childhood. That's what I'm sensing and that's why I
keep my feelings down."

After more eye movements, she said, "Dad is telling me that it
was true for the little girl but it doesn't have to be true for me
now. What I've been doing is making myself busy so I don't think
about these feelings of not feeling attached, of emotional
abandonment. That's been my coping strategy all along."

More eye movements and she closed her eyes. When she
opened them, Judy said thoughtfully, "The emotional
abandonment is too painful to feel. I'm glad that I could say it.
That explains a lot to me. I can put things in proper perspective
now. Those were childhood feelings. I now have a woman's
experience, knowledge and skills. I have compassion for the little
girl. I don't have the feelings of the little girl any longer. I am
centered and in the present. I will keep balance for today."

I said, "What would you like to ask your dad right now?" She
replied, "Why was it so hard for you to show love and
attachment? What happened to you?"

So I guided her through the eye movements and Judy closed
her eyes. After a few minutes, she opened them. "My father
wants me to accept and acknowledge that what he did for me
showed he was attached. 'Acceptance' he said. 'Acceptance of
what I did for you. Look at how I took care of you. I built houses.
I went to work every day. I tended a garden. I was very attached
to you. I gave you everything I had.'" She paused for a moment
and said, "Rochelle, now I realize I had never understood that
before."

I guided her through more eye movements and Judy closed
her eyes. When she opened them, she said, "Dad says he's
making no judgment. He says his emotional distance was the safe
way for him. It felt familiar for him because that was his
childhood experience."

After a final set of eye movements, she opened her eyes, smiling. "He just wants me to understand and accept what he was able to do. It's a whole bundle of acceptance. I am able to accept that now."

Life Changes from the Repair & Reattachment Grief Therapy

Judy's Repair & Reattachment Grief Therapy changed the disturbance she felt about her father's death. When Judy began her session, she said that the memory of leaving her father at the care-home was an 8.5. At the end of the session, she said it was a 0.

Judy's dad connected with her for over an hour. As she left, Judy said, "I'm so, so happy."

Craig's Grandma Draper

"We had to leave. Nothing can live forever."

– Grandma Draper to Craig during his connection

Craig is the author of *Your Eternal Self,*[3] and co-author of this book. Today. When we first began corresponding about this enhanced procedure for using bilateral stimulation to help people have perceived connections, he wanted to learn how the Repair & Reattachment Grief Therapy procedure is different from other such therapies. So he had me perform the procedure with him. This chapter contains a description of what happened.

Craig chose to focus on his grandma. "I was her favorite grandchild, the apple of her eye," he said. "I spent every summer with her since I was three years old. She would dote on me,

 squeezing coins into my little hands, taking me fishing, and lovingly frying the tiny, bony fish I caught. When it was time to leave at the end of the summer, she would cry and hug me goodbye. I would say, 'Don't cry Grandma. Someday I'll come and live with you forever.'

"I didn't have such a close relationship with my mother and father. My father was closed up emotionally. He never said to my mother, 'I love you,' in their married lives while I was a child, and I saw no affection between them. It seemed as though my father was always angry with me, and I didn't understand why. My mother was depressive, caught in a marriage that wasn't warm and loving. She felt bad that my father showed his anger toward me so much, but could do nothing about it.

"And so, I relished my summers with my openly loving, warm Grandma. But since I was closed up emotionally from my sterile home life, I couldn't really reciprocate her love as much as I now wish I had.

"When she was in her 80s, Grandma developed Alzheimer's. I can remember her sitting in the hospital with a blank smile on her face. She didn't know me, so I didn't visit very often. Then, one day she simply passed away. By that time, I hadn't had a connection with her for a while, so I felt sad, but wasn't overwhelmed with grief.

"I was living in my grandma and grandpa's house because Grandpa had moved out of the house into a nursing home two years before. He, Grandma, my mother, and her siblings had lived in the house for 60 years. Essentially, I had grown up in it as well, having lived there every summer of my childhood years. By the time of my grandparents' deaths, I had two lovely children, but they were living with my ex-wife, so I was alone in the house.

"A week or two after Grandma passed, my oldest uncle, the executor of my grandparents' estates, met with me in the house. I sat at the dining room table while he stood expressionless in front of me. He told me that Grandma had secretly left a substantial certificate of deposit for me. None of the other grandchildren were to know about it, and none of them had been left such a gift. My uncle sternly said he was unhappy that his children hadn't received a gift, and said that he and Grandpa had considered just not telling me about it. But they decided it was her wish, so they gave it to me. Grandma had pressed one last loving coin into my hand to let me know how much she loved me.

"Everything was fine with living in the house until Grandpa passed away. After his funeral, I was alone in that house filled with all the memories of my childhood with Grandma, and I just lost it. I was ranting through the house shouting, 'They're gone. They're gone. Grandma and Grandpa are gone.' I experienced the worst grieving I've had for any of my loved ones."

Craig sat in tears. It was the first time he had opened up these memories in decades.

The Repair & Reattachment Grief Therapy

After a few minutes, he said he was ready, and I began the Repair & Reattachment Grief Therapy procedure. The memory we started with was the image of his uncle talking with him sternly about the money Grandma had left for him. It was her last, surprising gesture of love toward him that she had carefully planned before developing Alzheimer's.

I said, "Keep that image and the words that go along with it in mind. Your uncle is talking to you sternly about the money Grandma had left for you." I had Craig follow my fingers, sweeping left and right in front of him, to perform the eye movement part of the Repair & Reattachment Grief Therapy procedure.

The connection began immediately. When he opened his eyes, he said, "I was in my Grandma and Grandpa's house, and I could see my uncle sternly talking to me. But behind him, smiling affectionately at me, I saw Grandma. She looked young, like I remember her from my childhood. She said to me, 'Don't listen to him, Craig.' Grandma and I walked out of the house onto the porch. As we sat on the old porch swing I had played on during my childhood, Grandma held my hand in her two hands."

I guided Craig through another set of eye movements and he described what he experienced. "I'm getting images now but they're not as vivid as what I just got." I checked to see how disturbing the image of his uncle's talking to him was. On a scale of 0 to 10, it had started out at a 9, but now he said "It's a zero." It was causing no disturbance.

I asked Craig to focus on another of the memories that was disturbing to him. He felt the other most disturbing memory was when he was in the house alone after his grandpa died and he "lost it." I had Craig follow my fingers, sweeping left and right in front of him as he focused on those words and the accompanying image. He closed his eyes and the connection happened immediately again. When he opened his eyes, he said, "I saw myself ranting through the house. 'They're gone,' I was shouting. But when I looked at the dining room table, there Grandma and Grandpa were sitting, both smiling warmly at me. 'We were there in the house with you the whole time,' Grandma said. They walked over to me and said, 'We had to leave. Nothing can live forever.' Then my uncle came in and said 'I'm sorry. I just didn't understand.' He gave me a hug."

I guided Craig through another set of eye movements. When he opened his eyes, he said, "It all changed, and I could see myself as a little boy playing on the living room floor in my grandma and grandpa's house, but they weren't with me. Then my mother and father came to me, looking very young, as they were when I was a child. They both knelt down with me and I got the message, 'We loved you too! We couldn't show it then, but **we love you now!**' Then my mom, dad, and I were walking outside of the house. Before the three of us was a panoramic view of vibrant green natural expanses, in bright sunlight. 'We have

many things to show you,' they said. 'You have work to do.' Then we were back in the living room and my whole family was there. 'We will guide you,' they said. There was a glow, an energy."

When Craig felt the communication with his family was finished, he said, "I'm going to ask whether any of our teams have anything to say to us." Craig believed that teams on the other side are working with us in our connections activities and writing. He felt they give guidance and arrange events to advance what we're doing in partnership with them to help individuals and humankind.

I guided Craig through the eye movements and he closed his eyes. When he opened them, he said, "I asked if the team members had anything to say to us. I got the impression that they were there, and heard 'You have work to do' again. Then I saw a large room with a long conference table. Seated all around it was an assemblage of many people, all smiling at me in greeting. It was clear to me they were the team members. At the end of the table was a large easel and pad, with intricate drawings and words on it. I heard, "It's all mapped out. The plans are already in place. All you have to do is follow them.'"

After another set of eye movements, Craig closed his eyes. When he opened them, he said, "I walked into the conference room and was shaking hands. I said, 'I feel so inadequate to be doing this.' I heard them say, 'You're not doing this alone. Keep the faith.' I said, 'Tell me what to do.' They said, "Just be open. Rochelle is an old soul. Stay with her. You were sent with a mission to do this work."

With those encouraging words, the session ended.

Life Changes from the Repair & Reattachment Grief Therapy

At the beginning of the session, Craig was in tears over the memories he hadn't recalled in decades. He rated his sadness at his uncle's stern talk with him as a 9, and of his ranting through the house after his grandma and grandpa were gone as a 10. Early in the Repair & Reattachment Grief Therapy, the sadness he felt when he brought to mind his uncle's talk with him had reduced to a 0. And later his memory of ranting through the house in grief that his grandma and grandpa were gone had changed to the image of them sitting at the dining room table smiling at him, saying "We were there the whole time." The memory no longer held any disturbance for him. It had reduced to a 0.

Craig's message from his parents helped him change his perspective on his early years with them, and the messages from the teams on the other side reassured him that we are on the right path. We just have to be open; the plan is already in place.

Audrey, Gary's Mom

"What's hard for you to understand, Gary, is that there isn't a separation between life and death."

-- Gary's mom, Audrey in his connection

Gary is a Washington State licensed psychotherapist certified in the use of EMDR, the most widely practiced method of bilateral stimulation used in counseling. I had known Gary for some time, and when I told him what I was experiencing in my office with Repair & Reattachment Grief Therapy, he was intrigued. We decided I would train him to facilitate the Repair & Reattachment Grief Therapy. Before I trained Gary, he had his own Repair & Reattachment Grief Therapy that I facilitated. This is the story of Gary's session to connect with his mother, Audrey, who passed into spirit in 2005 at 83 years of age.

"My mom was a model of unconditional love," Gary began. "I was cared for and loved. Mom was kind to a fault and gave to others freely, but was uncomfortable when someone wanted to give to her.

"At 51 years of age, she was diagnosed with multiple sclerosis. It made me very sad to see her suffer, especially on hot days. But she never let it get to her. It never stopped her. She would always keep going.

"Mom taught my brother and me, by word and example, that family must always love each other. Because of her model and love, our family has always been giving, and we have very warm relationships with each other.

"She was a strongly spiritual person and seemed to really enjoy her relationship with God. Everyone in the family knew that if they needed support from God, they could tell Audrey; she would get through.

"Mom loved the unlovable and didn't like to see people treated unjustly. She always saw the goodness in people.

"She was devoted to Dad and loved him deeply. I've never seen anyone in so much agony as she felt when my father died. She lost the will to live, and less than six months later, she went to be with him.

"The weakening that ended in her death really began soon after Dad died. Mom fell in the bathroom and hit the toilet, cracking some ribs. She was in great pain, and still grieving for

Dad. It was a hard time for her and for us watching her suffer. After that, nothing was the same.

"One Sunday while I was at a conference, I got a call from my cousin. Mom had had a stroke and was in the hospital. I returned home and rushed to the hospital. She was alert, and we talked warmly with each other. I told her all she meant to me and to all of us. True to form, she interrupted with a grin, 'Not so fast, I'm still here.'

"Mom was transferred to a rest home. One evening, I got a call from the rest home nurse. She said, 'Your mother has passed. She died about 10 minutes ago.' As I hung up the phone I was flooded with mixed feelings. 'You made it. You did it,' I said to myself, with a sense of relief that she was no longer in pain and was with Dad. But my sadness was strong. I wished that life had not been so physically hard for her. She suffered greatly.

"At the memorial service, I did the eulogy. It was easy to talk about how loving and how loved she was, because everyone seated there had been nurtured by the warmth of her care. Now it was time to honor her."

The Repair & Reattachment Grief Therapy

After Gary finished talking about his mom, we began the Repair & Reattachment Grief Therapy procedure. We chose the saddest thought he had about her passing. It was when she fell in the bathroom, cracking her ribs. While still grieving deeply for his dad, she was in terrible pain.

After the first set of eye movements focusing on that thought and the images accompanying it, he closed his eyes. When he opened them, he said that what came up was seeing her in the car coming back home from the hospital in discomfort. He felt very sad seeing her suffer. We continued the processing and his sadness decreased. Then he described uncomfortable physical sensations: tightness in his throat and pressure behind his eyes. With more processing, those feelings diminished.

Having relaxed away from the sadness and discomfort, the connection could unfold naturally. "The sadness is now shifting," he said after one set of eye movements. "I'm seeing lots of images flash before me. It's shifting, shifting, moving toward a sense of compassion. It feels right."

Gary opened his eyes after a set of eye movements and said, "I feel just a sense of her presence." The connection was beginning. I said, "Drop the 'just a' and go with what you're getting." I guided him through another set of eye movements and he closed his eyes. When he opened them, he said, "I sense her presence. I see a bright blue and have a nice relaxed feeling."

After another set of eye movements, Gary continued, "Plants, I see different plants and her voice says, 'Plants can nurture you too.' Then I could see the plants better and they were closer to me. Everything went away except a nice comfortable feeling. Then what I heard was 'A heart for healing.'"

I guided Gary through a set of eye movements and when he opened his eyes, he said, "Now, I'm getting a sensation of that color blue again, that spiritual color blue. I see her sitting in the house alone in her chair, with a sense of calm. We had a sunroom where the sun came in, making it warm."

I said, "Ask any question you want to ask your mom." Gary said, "I want to ask for energy, love, and strength to manifest through me." I said, "OK. You're in the sunroom with her. It's warm. Ask her the question." After a set of eye movements, he closed his eyes. When he opened them, he said, "I asked for energy, love and strength to manifest through me, and the message from Mom came in two parts: One, 'It always was, and it always will be.' And two, 'What's hard for you to understand, Gary, is that there isn't a separation between life and death.'"

Gary and I were both moved by this profoundly wise insight into life and death from his mom. With that, he felt that she had finished, so the Repair & Reattachment Grief Therapy ended.

Life Changes from the Repair & Reattachment Grief Therapy

Using the scale of disturbance strength from 0, meaning none, to 10, meaning very severely disturbing, at the beginning of the session, Gary rated several of his memories as 10s and some 8s.

He rated the memory of his mother's falling and cracking her ribs as a 10 plus. By the end of the session, he said that had reduced to a 2. The memory of his mom's life becoming full of pain from the cracked ribs and sadness after his dad died began as a 10. By the end of the session, he rated it a 0.

Joe, John's Brother

"You don't have to worry anymore. There's peace, and you're still connected."

John came to me grieving for his brother Joe, who had died four years previously at 59 years of age.

They grew up together, one year apart in age, in New York City. Their father died when John was four and a half years old and Joe was only three. Without a father, the boys became very close to each other.

"Joe was mad when our father died because he left him," John said. "The kids would ask, 'Where is your dad?' and we were just really embarrassed because we didn't know what to tell them.

"I grew up with my mom, my sister Elizabeth, and Joe. Joe and I hung out together when we were teenagers, had the same

 friends, and went to the same Catholic schools until we went to different high schools.

"We basically grew up in the streets of New York, playing tag, or cards, or games like checkers and chess. We would play stick ball in the street or handball against the wall. We'd flip cards and pitch pennies. The streets of New York were our place to have fun.

"Then, as we got to be around 18 or 19, Joe got pretty wild. He liked to go out and have a good time. We wouldn't go far from our little neighborhood. There was a bar on every corner, and if we weren't at a bar, we were hanging out at someone's house.

"After high school, Joe went into the Marines and I went into the Air Force. When he was discharged from the Marines, Joe became a New York City cop for a long time. Then, in 1982, he had a car accident and was in a coma for about a month. When he came out of the coma, Joe was different. He was quiet when we were growing up, but after the coma, he was more talkative, and he had lost his sense of smell. He was in the hospital for a while after he came out of his coma. I visited him all the time.

"I moved to Washington in 1989. Joe moved to Florida a few years later. Then, in 2006, his wife called me and explained tearfully that Joe had stopped breathing a few hours earlier. She had called the EMTs, but they took a wrong turn and didn't arrive at their house for a long time. She explained that his son Mike was trying to give him CPR, but couldn't revive him. They drove to the hospital, but by the time they arrived, he was gone. We found out later, after the autopsy, that his heart was so heavily damaged that he couldn't have survived even if they had gotten him to the hospital right away.

"I called my sister Elizabeth. When I told her Joe was dead, she started screaming on the phone. We were really close, Joe, Elizabeth, and me.

"We were all crying at the wake. Joe's daughter Linda was really devastated. She was daddy's little girl. It's been four years now, but when I talk to Linda or Joe's wife, Grace, we usually don't bring him up. Today is the anniversary of Joe's death. I called Grace yesterday, and she said 'Don't call me tomorrow.' I feel the same grief. That's why I'm here."

The Repair & Reattachment Grief Therapy

When John finished telling me about his brother Joe, we began the Repair & Reattachment Grief Therapy process. He decided that the saddest memory was being at the wake with everybody. I asked him how sad that made him feel on a scale of 0 to 10 with 10 being the saddest. He said, "10 plus, plus, plus."

I asked him to focus on the image of Linda at the wake with the thought, "She was daddy's little girl" and guided him through a set of eye movements. He closed his eyes. When he opened them, he said, "I saw a bright light on top of my head to the right. I felt pretty peaceful. There was some red on the left side. Then I was hovering over a big space. I saw clouds and soft pillows."

We did several more sets of eye movements, followed by his descriptions of what he experienced with his eyes closed. Then, after a set he said, "I'm in a large area and I feel peaceful. It's all opening up, a white area, open wide, all open on the right.

There's a big yellow bench with a sofa, but nobody's on it. It's weird! Now I can see my brother, my mother, my dad, and a bench. There's a presence above the bench. I see everything bright yellow on my right side."

After more sets of eye movements, he said, "I heard Billy Joel playing music in the background. Oh my gosh, that's what Joe loved, Billy Joel, and that music was playing in the background at his wake."

We did more processing and John continued, "Now I'm at the wake. We loosened Joe's tie. He hated ties. Just now I heard him saying, 'Thanks for loosening my tie.' Joe just left the wake. That's what I'm getting. He just left the wake."

I asked him, "On a scale of 0 to 10, how is your sadness now when you think about Joe's daughter, Linda, at the wake?" John looked away briefly and said, "When I think of the wake now, my sadness is a zero. It was a 10 plus, plus, plus, but now it's a zero, nothing. I feel peaceful . . . and tired."

We did more eye movements. After he opened his eyes, John described what he experienced: "The message I got was 'I'm around. You don't have to ask my advice. It'll just be there.' Joe said to me, 'You know what I would say. You don't have to ask me. Just listen to it.' Then I saw Mom and Joe. They were both telling me they'll always be there."

With that, the connection ended. I asked John how he felt about what happened. He replied, "There's this link. They are always around. This is okay. Things are okay. They give you a peace being there. You don't have to worry anymore. You don't miss them as much. There's peace, and you're still connected."

As he left, John said he was very, very happy.

Life Changes from the Repair & Reattachment Grief Therapy

At the beginning of the session, I asked John his ratings, on the scale of 0 to 10, for how disturbing four memories were for him: his sister-in-law's calling to say Joe wasn't breathing, feeling embarrassed as a young boy to say to people their dad had died, his sister's screaming when she heard the news Joe was dead, and seeing Joe's daughter Linda devastated at the wake. He rated them all as 10 plus, plus, plusses before the session—-they were very disturbing for him. When he rated the memories during the session, he said their effects on him had all diminished to 0—no disturbance.

I talked to John four weeks later and asked him, "How are you doing?" He said buoyantly, "I'm doing good! I'm laughing a lot more. I have a connection! And I feel good! Do you think things are going to change for me, Rochelle? Because you said that. It changes lives." I said, "Yes! Just be open to it. Let it come to you. Just be open and be aware."

Elizabeth's Grandma Lily

"It's all a game, a drama we play out, but in the end, its essence is love."

– Elizabeth's Grandma Lily Hanson, in her connection

Elizabeth wanted to do a session connecting with her
Grandma Lily Hanson, who died at age 62. "Grandma Hanson
had three sons," Elizabeth told me. "Dad was the middle son.
When Dad was 16, Grandma left Grandpa for another man. After
that, the house felt empty to Dad, and he carried a lot of
resentment toward her.

"I was her first granddaughter after four grandsons. She used
to tell Mom, 'Elizabeth is going to live with me when she turns
12.' Mom would say, 'Over my dead body.'

"Grandma didn't live to see me turn 12. I was only 10 when
Mom told me Grandma had been diagnosed with cancer. Soon
after, Grandma came and stayed with us in a room upstairs, next
to my room. Every day, she took the streetcar to work where she
sewed drapes. At the end of the day, I would meet her at the
streetcar and walk home with her. I would stay in her room and
talk to her while she cooked her supper on a hot plate. We talked
about sewing, and Grandma told me she had a sewing machine
she wanted me to have when she died.

"After a few months, she got really sick from the cancer. Mom
wasn't home during the day to take care of her, so she moved in
with my aunt, who could be home all day to care for her because
my aunt didn't work.

"Soon, Grandma had to go to the hospital and stay as she
grew sicker. While Grandma was in the hospital, I went to an
Evangelical Church and gave my heart to Jesus. I was only 10
years old. I thought Jesus could heal my grandma. There was a
contest to see how many new people any of us could bring to
church. I really worked at telling people to come to church, and
brought in 54 new people. I won the contest. I was sure a great
miracle was going to happen so Grandma wouldn't die. But right
after I won the contest, Grandma died.

"Only a month or two later, I was awakened by the phone
ringing in the middle of the night. I heard my mother screaming.
Aunt Mary, my mom's sister, had died."

With that, Elizabeth ended her description of her Grandma Lily Hanson, and we began the Repair & Reattachment Grief Therapy procedure.

The Repair & Reattachment Grief Therapy

Elizabeth said the most disturbing memory she had was when the phone rang in the middle of the night and her mother was screaming that Aunt Mary had died. I told her to keep that image and the thoughts that go along with it in mind. I guided her through a set of eye movements and she closed her eyes. After a short time, she opened them and described what came to her: "I saw myself going to my aunt and uncle's house for Aunt Mary's funeral. Her body is in a casket in the living room. My uncle and cousins, Aunt Mary's children, were there."

After another set of eye movements, Elizabeth opened her eyes and said the scene had changed. "I kept hearing, 'Lizzie, Lizzie.' That's what Grandma called me. I saw Grandma sitting by a tree on a white blanket. She wanted me to come over there to her, but I couldn't seem to get there."

We did another set of eye movements. Elizabeth opened her eyes and said, "I was sitting by Grandma. I'm a little girl and my dad and uncles are there. There seems to be a barrier. She and my dad are crying. They're all close, surrounded by love. They have healed all the hurt. What I'm getting is, 'It's all a game, a drama we play out, but in the end its essence is love. Love and connection are all that matters. The rest is just a game.' And I heard the words over and over, 'Love and connections. Over here, there's just love and connections.'"

With that message, Elizabeth felt they had finished the connection, so we ended the session.

Life Changes from the Repair & Reattachment Grief Therapy

At the end of the session, I asked Elizabeth about the memories she had rated as being highly disturbing at the beginning. She said they had all reduced to zeroes.

Marj, Michael's Mom

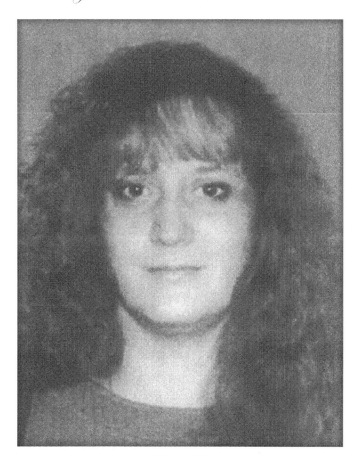

"*She's saying I should let go of the past and move forward.*"

– Message from Marj, Michael's mom, in his connection

Michael's mother, Marj, was only 33 years old when she died. Michael was 12 at the time. When he had his Repair & Reattachment Grief Therapy session with me, he was 20.

"She had a very likeable personality," he said. "Everyone loved her. We always had fun grocery shopping. I got to help find things on the grocery list, like a scavenger hunt. Then I helped put the groceries away.

"When I was little, in the evening after dinner, she would sit on the floor and play games with me, and she would sing me a good night song—"Good Night Sweetheart." We'd go out to do errands together and along the way, we'd play 'I Spy' games and license-plate alphabet.

"When I had nightmares, she would come into my room and sing to me. My mom was my best friend.

"Then Mom started having a lot of pain and one kidney infection after another. They couldn't figure out what was wrong. After a while, they found out that she had some form of cancer, but they couldn't find out what kind. So she went through radiation and chemotherapy.

"Mom basically lived in the hospital. She would come home from the hospital, then have to go back. I went with her sometimes when I wasn't in school. I was in the sixth grade. Every once in a while, I was called out of class to go to the counseling office. My dad would be there. He was staying with my mom in the hospital, so he would come to my school to tell me what was going on with her.

"A month before my mom passed away, she was pretty much dead already. She didn't remember me, my dad, or my sisters. She didn't know who anyone was, even herself.

"She passed away in the hospital in my dad's arms. My sister and I were at home when it happened. When my dad came home from the hospital, my sister Jackie was on the couch and I was coming out of the shower. Dad just stood there with his head hung down and didn't say anything. We knew.

"My dad, my sisters, and I all got to see her in the casket the day before the funeral. We all bawled our eyes out. At the funeral, I stood there and held her hand and talked to her. I told her, 'Mom, I love you. Thank you for being my mom.' After a while, they made me stand back and they closed the casket. That's when I actually realized my mom was gone. I broke down crying. I was crying while I helped my dad carry her casket. I promised Mom I would do it. I was only 12.

"After the funeral, everyone went down to the town where we lived and we had a memorial for my mom. We played her favorite songs, like 'The Wind Beneath My Wings' by Bette Midler. Then we all went home.

"One night, I had a dream about my mom. I was in the living room with Dad, and Mom was there. I gave them both a hug. I told her how much I loved her and how much I missed her. She flashed us, like a big white light! My mom said to me, 'It's time to wake up,' and I woke up. That's all I thought about for a week. I even wrote a poem about it: 'Forget Me Not.' I got an A in my class for it.

"For a long time after Mom died, I did drugs. I don't do drugs anymore. I am 20 now, and I am getting my life together for the first time in a long, long time, trying to figure out who I am and my place in the world."

The Repair & Reattachment Grief Therapy

After Michael finished telling me about his mom, whom he loved so dearly and missed so desperately, I began the Repair & Reattachment Grief Therapy procedure.

I asked him to rate the most disturbing memory on the scale of 0 to 10. It was when they closed the casket and he fully realized his mom was gone. He was only 12 years old. We started with this memory. When I asked him how disturbing it was on a scale of 0 to 10, he said it was a 10.

The second most disturbing memory was when Michael broke down crying, but helped his dad carry his mom's casket as he had promised his mom he would do. He rated its disturbance at a 9.

After the first set of eye movements, Michael closed his eyes. When he opened them, he said, "I'm re-living it. I'm seeing it happen again from an outside point of view, not the feelings. Now it helps me see that's why my dad and I are so close today." For each of three more sets of eye movements, he was getting no new impressions. I asked him their impact on him on a scale of 0 to 10, with 0 being no impact and 10 being very strong sadness. The most disturbing memory, of when the casket was closed and he realized she was gone, had reduced from a 9 to a 2. The second memory, of helping his dad carry his mom's casket, had reduced from a 9 to a 1.

As I continued the procedure, it became clear that reducing Michael's sadness when he thought about the saddening memories would be a primary outcome of this Repair & Reattachment Grief Therapy session.

I had Michael focus on a third memory he had that made him feel very sad. It was remembering that a month before his mom's death, she was pretty much dead already; she didn't know anyone. After the sets of eye movements, Michael described images of her not knowing anyone. I asked about the sadness for that image, and on the scale of 0 to 10, that memory had dropped from 8 to a 0.

So we started with another feeling: Michael felt he had failed to keep the family together after his mom's death because he pretty much gave up and fell into using drugs. He rated the disturbance level of that memory as an 8. After another series of eye movements and his describing impressions related to that feeling, I checked his sadness connected to it and it had fallen to a 0.

During these sets of procedures and the effects they were having of reducing his sadness, I could see Michael progressively relaxing. Next, I asked him to focus on the dream he had about his mother after her death and I guided him through a set of eye movements. He closed his eyes. When he opened them, he said, "I'm re-dreaming the dream." I said, "What question do you want to ask your mom?" Michael said, "Are you proud of me, Mom?" So we did another set of eye movements and the connection began. When he opened his eyes, he smiled broadly and told me, "She said she is proud of me. She said I should let go of the past and move forward."

After more eye movements, Michael remarked that he could still feel her presence. I said, "Ask if there is anything else she wants to say to you before we are done." I guided him through the eye movements and he closed his eyes. When he opened them, he reported, "Mom said, 'Keep working hard.' She told me she loves me. She said she's happy, and she's pleased that I am making better decisions now." Then the connection was done.

Michael said to me, "I feel calm and relaxed. She was saying the words to me. I felt her presence like when I'm dreaming."

Life Changes from the Repair & Reattachment Grief Therapy

When the session started, Michael rated the sadness he felt as he remembered when they closed the casket and he realized his mom was gone as a 10. It reduced to a 2. The memory that a month before she passed away, she was pretty much dead started as an 8. It reduced to a 0. The distress of the memory that he felt he had failed to keep the family together started as an 8. At the end of the session, it was a 0.

I saw Michael a few weeks later. He explained that he's been doing much better. I said, "When you bring up thoughts of your mom, how do you feel?" He said, "I'm not upset anymore. I feel my mom's presence and I'm not sad anymore. I feel OK."

Michael is looking forward to his future. His mom told him he should let go of the past and move forward. He has enrolled in a community college, something he felt he would never do, and plans to go on for a 4-year degree.

Emma's Grandma Jane

"Love yourself with a
vengeance. Do not live your
life in fear. I will always be
behind the light."

– Grandma Jane to Emma during her connection

"My grandma was murdered in 1988," Emma began. "She was 87 years old.

"Grandma was the rock of the family. She was very strong and had more energy than someone half her age. Grandma had a lot of community friends and family, but she wasn't touchy-feely normally, except when she was with me. We had a very special relationship, one that my mother and I did not have. I loved Grandma.

"When I was little, Grandma would make me clothes. There were no store labels on them, of course. One day I noticed the other kids' clothes had labels on them, and I asked her, 'Why aren't there labels on my clothes?' So, she put labels on the clothes she made for me to keep me from feeling I was different from the other children. Grandma would really listen to me. I could tell by things she did how much she loved me.

"As a teenager I drifted away from Grandma. I felt bad about it, but being a typical teen, I didn't have enough time for her. I remember when I was 16 I had a car accident and called her for help. I felt bad I hadn't spoken to her for a long time. I asked her for a loan to fix my car, and she gave it to me. I said to Grandma, 'I'll pay you back,' but she wasn't concerned. She was so gracious. And I did pay back the estate after she was killed, to show my love and respect.

"On Mother's Day in May 1988, we had arranged for my sister, Mom, Grandma, and my other grandmother, Grandma Jane, to go out for Mother's Day. I was really excited to see Grandma. Early on Mother's Day, we were all dressed and ready to go when we received a distressing phone call. Police found the back door of Grandma's garage kicked in, and she had been kidnapped. The kidnappers had taken her car, but the police had no clues about who had done it or where they had taken her. She didn't have her medicine or her glasses.

"We drove straight down to Grandma's house. There were police everywhere. They let my mom into the house, and she looked for the Black Hills Gold ring Grandma had. Mom knew I always admired it and wanted to see if it had been stolen. She found the ring and brought it out to me. I wore it for years. It became my only link to Grandma.

"For a harrowing month, we heard nothing. Finally, my mom received a phone call from a detective. They had found Grandma's body in the woods on a military reservation outside of town. She had been shot in both legs and the head, execution style. The detective said she had a very peaceful look and was kind of looking up at the sun when they found her.

"They also said all three of the murderers had been caught, and he was sure they would spend their lives behind bars. But that didn't matter. Grandma was dead."

The Repair & Reattachment Grief Therapy

When Emma finished telling me her story, we began the Repair & Reattachment Grief Therapy procedure. The most distressing memory for her was when they drove to Grandma's house and police were everywhere. She had been excited to see Grandma, but she was gone.

The connection began very quickly, after the first set of eye movements. Emma opened her eyes and said, "I heard, 'I'll always be behind the light. Your choice is to live in the dark or the light.'"

I led her through more eye movements and she closed her eyes. When she opened them, she said, "I saw a dark hole, a dark box, and felt a struggle, then a sense of peace. I felt a weight on my shoulders and I couldn't breathe. Then I saw a bright light, and grandma started coming through. Grandma said to me, 'Don't get me wrong, Emma, I fought to the end. You over-think things, Emma. Life is simple. Fear not that I'm standing next to you. I will not carry you but I will be standing next to you. Fear not. I will make you see. I am happy where I am. I am at peace.'"

After more eye movements, she closed her eyes. When she opened them, she said, "I saw an image of Grandma before she was killed and heard her saying, 'Don't you see? It's all about closure. Fear is what is deadly, not what happened to me. I was not afraid. You need to see and feel what I feel for me to be able to help you."

We did more eye movements and when Emma opened her eyes, she said, "Grandma said 'Come on. Come on.' I asked, 'How?' I felt that Grandma was a little agitated. She said, 'I will guide you if you just listen, and then you will see that fear is deadly. Fear is deadly and it is killing you. What you are doing to yourself is worse than what happened to me. You're living in a state of paralysis, and I fought to the end. They paralyzed me and left me for dead, but they didn't win. I did."

After another set of eye movements and a brief period with her eyes closed, Emma opened them and said, "I asked Grandma, 'How do I keep fear from controlling my life?' And what came through from Grandma was, 'You block yourself. Don't you see believing in yourself is the answer? Believing in yourself is what overcomes fear. Know what you stand for without wavering. That is what creates peace. At the end, those men paralyzed me. I fought to the end and I knew where I was going, not that I wanted to go, but I knew it was the end. You were born fearful, but you will overcome it. It's a process.'"

At that point, we had gone three hours. I was tired and I could see that Emma was tired. I asked Emma to ask Grandma if it was OK to stop now and reconvene tomorrow. I guided her through the eye movements and she closed her eyes. When she opened them, she said "I asked Grandma, 'Is it OK to stop now and reconvene tomorrow?' Grandma answered, 'Honey, I'm not going anywhere and we have work to do. It's time to pull up those bootstraps. OK? I'm going to make you see. There is more work to do and you will get closure. You will see.'"

Emma shook her head and smiled, "That was the way she always talked to me. There was no nonsense about Grandma."

Emma's Second Session

Emma came back for a session the next day. She began by explaining that her ex-husband had contacted her three days ago. She said she had been having problems in threes. Three years ago, she left her husband. Three months ago, she had her divorce. And three days ago, her ex-husband contacted her. "That's my problem in threes," she said.

When she was ready, we began the Repair & Reattachment Grief Therapy procedure. After a set of eye movements, Emma closed her eyes, focusing on Grandma. She had them closed for a long time. When she opened them, she said, "I'm so tired. I'm like so tired."

We did another set of eye movements and Emma closed her eyes. This time she opened them after a short time. She said, "I saw a light and heard Grandma saying, 'Emma, you're just not seeing it. Don't you see I'm right behind the light? I know you are tired. Don't give up now. Focus. Let's get to work. You have so many distractions. I am behind the light so starting asking questions. There are three rules in life: past, present, future. Forget the past, look to the future and know that now, I am behind the light. There are two things you need to understand. One, I am a metaphor for your life: the big black hole and the trunk of the car that I was in.' I said, 'For me?' But Grandma just continued. 'That's how you have been living your life. The black hole was too late for me. It's not too late for you. You need to get out of it.'

"Then Grandma said, 'Two, love yourself with a vengeance. Do not live your life in fear. I will always be behind the light. Live by these rules and you will be complete. Three months, three days, three years, it's all over.' She knew about my problems coming in threes. Then she said, 'It's a symbol: the pain, anxiety, and fear are over. Release, Emma; it's time. It's time to release your fear, your pain and your anxiety. Release it. We are all behind the light. The light is on your path. All you need to do is follow it. We are with you by your side as you go down your path. We can't do it for you, but you will do it. It's all about getting out of the black hole and letting go of the past. Fear will not dictate your anxiety; your passions will.'

"I said, 'Wow,' and Grandma just kept on. 'Live passionately. Be happy. That is the definition of success. Fear not. I will always be behind the light. OK. You got it. It's time to do it. Live the way I've outlined for you.'"

We did another set of eye movements and Emma closed her eyes. When she opened her eyes, she said, "Grandma said to me, 'Emma, do this. One, go home, make tapioca pudding, and warm your soul. Two, trust in the process. You need to work on your fears and you will be done. Go back to what we started on and you will understand your fear. Live in the dark or live in the light, it's a choice. I can't do it for you but I can show you the way. The right answers always carry an underlying sense of peace, the wrong path, an underlying sense of anxiety. There's the dark and there is the light and that is your choice. We are on the lighted path. Go down the lighted path. The past is done. Go down the path that is lit. It's time to let go of me in this world. I'll always be behind the light. Trust in your transformation. You will find peace and happiness. I am at peace.'"

We did another set of eye movements and Emma closed her eyes. Grandma continued, "'You're tired, Emma. Make tapioca pudding. Put yourself into my feather bed and trust the path. I will always be there, and here.' Then it went dark. I know Grandma is done for now."

Emma explained, "Grandma used to make me tapioca pudding when I was a little girl and put me in her feather bed. It made me feel secure and loved. So, she is saying to me, "When you make tapioca pudding, and lay in my feather bed, trust the path. I'll be there."

Life Changes from the Repair & Reattachment Grief Therapy

The most distressing memory for Emma at the beginning of the session was when they drove to Grandma's house and police were everywhere. Grandma was gone. By the end of the session, her rating of that memory's disturbance for her had reduced to a zero—no disturbance.

I saw Emma three days after the session. She walked into my office smiling and sat down. I said, "How are you doing, Emma?" She said, "I have a sense of happiness I haven't had for a long,

long time. I feel peaceful and calm. And I know Grandma is at peace. I feel a connection with her that I haven't felt before.

"I went out and bought new clothes. I went down to the salon and had my hair cut and fixed. I just have this inner peace and relaxation."

We did a brief Repair & Reattachment Grief Therapy session. After the eye movements, she closed her eyes. When she opened them, she said, "I heard Grandma's voice say 'Emma, you can be whatever you want to be.' But I felt a little bit of fear and anxiety thinking about the future."

I said to Emma, "Keep that in mind and go back." I guided her through a set of eye movements and she closed her eyes. When she opened them, she said, "I saw a big black ball, and then the big black ball blew up. I heard the word 'Renewal.'"

Emma ended the session by saying, "Rochelle, I have become a powerful and self-assured woman."

Postscript

During the session Emma's grandma said "The right answers always carry an underlying sense of peace, the wrong path an underlying sense of anxiety." After the session, I thought to myself, how profound that is! People should use this in their lives as a guide.

Sam, Deidre's Ex-husband

"The important thing is to finish what you're doing. You'll have all the help you need."

– Deidre's ex-husband, Sam, in her connection

Deidre is a nurse practitioner I have known for some time. She wanted to experience the Repair & Reattachment Grief Therapy procedure, so I did a session with her. The account of her session follows.

Deidre began telling me about her ex-husband, Sam, who died when he was 50. "Sam sold Cadillacs," she said. "I met him when he was showing a car to my boyfriend. He walked across the car dealership lot and it was love at first sight. He was holding my hand behind my boyfriend's back. He proposed two weeks later, and within three months, we ran off to Las Vegas and got married. We didn't tell anyone. During our marriage, we had two boys and a girl: Greg, Troy, and Lisa.

"Sam was very handsome and charming, but extremely manipulative. He was an alcoholic and became physically abusive with me three or four times. He had affairs with other women our entire marriage. After years of affairs and abuse toward me and my children, I divorced him.

"I thought about Sam often after the divorce, and four years later, I sat alone in my bedroom reading through all the letters he had written me, crying for what I had lost, in spite of the abuse. I looked at all the old pictures of Sam and me in happier days, one by one, crying the entire time. After hours of reminiscing, I had the liberating experience of forgiving Sam. That was at about 7:30 p.m. The next day, I learned that Sam had killed himself at that time the previous evening.

"I got the call that Sam had killed himself while I was at the office. Mary, my friend, was in the office when I heard the news. She drove me to tell our children. 'How am I going to tell the kids?' I thought, still in shock.

"When I told each child about their father's death, I found they already knew. I think they were in shock.

"I learned that his current wife, Polly, had discovered him with a fatal gunshot wound to the head. She said he committed suicide, but I was suspicious of Polly. Sam was court ordered to keep an insurance policy on himself that named our children as beneficiaries so they would continue to be supported if he died.

Two weeks before his death, Polly changed the policies so she would get all of the money in the event he died. To add to my suspicions, police first said a suicide note was found, but later said no suicide note had been found.

But in spite of Polly's changing the life insurance policies just weeks before Sam's suspicious death, police never investigated it. A friend and business colleague of Sam's was also suspicious and hired a private investigator to look into Sam's death. The private investigator took the case and was working on it, but then mysteriously stopped returning our phone calls. He just dropped out of the case with no explanation. We never did find out what really happened."

The Repair & Reattachment Grief Therapy

When Deidre had finished telling me about Sam, I began the Repair & Reattachment Grief Therapy procedure. I asked her what the most disturbing memory was, and she said it was when she had just learned about Sam's death and was thinking, "How am I going to tell my kids?"

I guided Deidre through a set of eye movements. She closed her eyes, focusing on the image and feelings that accompanied the thought, "How am I going to tell my kids?" When she opened them, she said she saw herself telling Troy about Sam's death.

Throughout the next 45 minutes of eye movements and experiences, many memories came up: some very positive and some not so positive. Finally, after a set of eye movements, she closed her eyes and the connection began.

When Deidre opened her eyes, she said "Now, I'm floating in water. I'm snorkeling. I see Sam huddled way down in a corner of the ocean, afraid to come out. I'm telling him, 'It's OK.' I see him, but he's not talking to me."

After another set of eye movements, Deidre said, "Sam was a tortured soul and I keep hearing the words 'Too dangerous, too dangerous.' I sense he's talking about the mystery surrounding his death. I see him sitting on the floor of the ocean in a ball. I have my arms around him saying, 'It's OK. It's OK.'"

I guided her through another set of eye movements and
Deidre closed her eyes. She had them closed a very long time,
probably 15 minutes or more. Finally she opened them and said,
"It's like he's stuck. I go over to him and tell him that I forgive
him. 'The kids forgive you,' I say."

After another set of eye movements, Deidre closed her eyes.
With her eyes still closed, she exclaimed, "Sam's saying, 'She
killed me. She killed me.'" I, Rochelle, felt a huge rush of
emotions and chills across my body. I got goose bumps. Deidre
continued, "There was struggling with a gun . . . and then the
image went away. That's all I got."

Following a few more sets of eye movements, Deidre said, "I
asked him about the grandchildren. He's so into our little
grandson Jay. We sort of had a conversation. We talked about
our granddaughter Kayla. Sam said he is watching over Kayla
and Jay."

After more eye movements, Deidre said "Sam needed my
forgiveness to come out of that space, that ball, as a tortured soul.
I went to where he was hiding in a ball and pulled him up from
the bottom of the ocean. We swam to shore. I led him to a bench
and said, 'Let's sit down on this park bench.' So Sam and I are
sitting on the bench talking about our grandchildren. His hair is
messy, so unlike his perfectly stylized hair in life. He's so much
more relaxed and happy now."

We did another set of eye movements. After Deidre opened
her eyes, she said, "I could see my guides dancing. They knew
they were close enough to catch me if I fell in any direction. They
said, 'We are always here to hold you up.'"

Deidre continued, "I wanted to see my niece Jill, my friend
Marty, and my mom and dad. I did see them off in the distance. I
was getting a glimpse of each one of them." Soon after that, the
session ended.

Second Session Connecting with Sam

Deidre came back to have another session. She said that after
the first session, she spent an evening looking through pictures of

her ex-husband, Sam. That night she had a dream of him. In the dream, he came back to her. But she didn't care if he left or stayed. Deidre explained, "I was wondering if he was going to leave. I saw him looking into a mirror in the bathroom. I didn't want him to leave, though. I wanted things to be the way they were for our family, but not the bad parts. I wanted a functional relationship. I didn't want him drinking. I just wanted the good parts."

Deidre and I then began the Repair & Reattachment Grief Therapy procedure to make another connection with Sam. We used the dream as the focus. Deidre wore the headphones as I guided her through a set of eye movements and she closed her eyes. When she opened them, she said, "I was flashing on good memories. Then Sam and I were walking down the beach like we're making up. I'm holding Sam's hand. He sat down in the sand and I asked him, 'Is there anything you want me to tell the kids?' He said, 'Tell Greg I am so very proud of him. Greg is everything he could have been. Tell Troy what a wonderful father he is. I'm really sorry I was so hard on Lisa. I know I stifled her creativity.' Then Sam started sobbing and said, 'I'm sorry for how I treated you. It made you a stronger person and I'm proud of that. It's time for things to get better for you and for you to be happy.'"

After another set of eye movements, Deidre closed her eyes and sat quietly for a while. When she opened her eyes, she told me, "Sam said a lot of things. He looked like he did when he was young, with his hair hanging down. He had on white pants and a white top, like a karate suit. But there was no belt on the karate suit. Sam sat on a bench and I sat next to him. He said to me, 'The most important thing you must work on is your book with Martha.' I'm co-authoring a book about our work relating to the body and medicine. Sam said to me, 'Concentrate on the victimhood part to help people live healthier lives. I was a prime example of what blaming does to the body. Keep working with Martha because you work well together and motivate each other.'"

We did another set of eye movements, and after she opened her eyes, Deidre continued: "He talked to me about promoting my book. He said to me, 'I have a much larger perspective from the other side.'"

We did another set of eye movements and Deidre described what came to her: "I have a guide named Alison. Sam says Alison and the other guides around me are propping me up. Then I saw an image of everyone propping me up. Alison was saying, 'Put one foot in front of the other. It will all work out.'

"I started telling Sam about my concerns for each of my kids. He said, "Deidre, they are grown now. They need to live their own lives. It's their affairs now; don't interfere with them.'"

I guided her through another set of eye movements. She continued describing her connection with Sam. "We walked around the garden. We stopped and Sam hugged me. Despite all the problems we had, we created three beautiful souls and two beautiful grandchildren. He said to me, 'You need to set a good example and get it together financially again. You need to finish what you're here to do. The important thing for you is to finish what you're doing. You'll have all the help you need, and you'll be able to buy that damn house if you want it.' He was laughing. I'm renting the house I'm living in now but I want to buy it."

We did another set of eye movements and Deidre closed her eyes. When she opened them, she explained, "Sam said to me, 'There's lots of really good life left, and you'll have all the strength that you need to do it.' Then he said to me, 'Thanks for pulling me up from the bottom of the ocean.'"

After another set of eye movements, Deidre said, "Now we are dancing in the garden. 'I can dance!' I said. Sam said to me, 'Put humor in the book.'"

Because Sam was so forthcoming with information, I said to Deidre, "Ask Sam if there is anything he has to say about the Repair & Reattachment Grief Therapy work I'm doing." I guided her through a set of eye movements and she closed her eyes. After a few moments, she opened them, smiling. "Sam said to me, 'Obviously I like it because I'm talking to you, and I got pulled out from the bottom of the ocean. What Rochelle is doing is very important work in conjunction with all the changes the world is going through. Rochelle was chosen to do it because she has the heart, the skills, and the disposition to do it. It's her path, and she'll grow tremendously from what she's going to be asked to do. It's really big. Appearing on national television talk shows isn't such a long shot.'" We both laughed.

Deidre continued, "Sam has this huge presence. He said, 'Deidre, your book will fulfill its purpose. It's going to help a lot of people but it doesn't have to have the mass appeal that Rochelle's book does. It will do what it is supposed to do. You will have help along the way. Don't be a skeptic.'

"Rochelle, I have a feeling he really is around and he will be around in a much more positive form, all the time, to help and support me."

With that, we ended the session.

Third Session Connecting with Sam

A few days later, Deidre came back for another session. I began the Repair & Reattachment Grief Therapy procedure and she immediately went back into her connection with Sam. She asked many questions about her life and the direction she was going in. Sam answered every question, giving her one after another remarkably relevant, insightful suggestion.

After one set of eye movements, Deidre closed her eyes and asked Sam what her involvement in facilitating Repair & Reattachment Grief Therapy and working with me might be. When she opened her eyes, she reported that Sam told her, "You're not ready to know yet what it's about. Your involvement is going to work into this in a way that will really surprise you and Rochelle. Yes, you should be trained by Rochelle. Yes, you will be doing it, but neither of you have thought of this unusual way of using this procedure. There are other, more extensive uses for it. You will be using it with a part of the spirit that is still alive."

Soon after that intriguing revelation, we ended the session.

Life Changes from the Repair & Reattachment Grief Therapy

When Deidre began her first session, she had a number of memories that she rated as being very disturbing: 10s and "high 10s." After the procedure, I asked her about the memories. She said, "All the 10s are not a problem. They're zeroes now."

Peggy's Mom

"I love you. I always will be with
you. Marilyn is being taken care
of. Just love her."

– Peggy's mom in her connection

Peggy's mom died a year before Peggy came to see me. "My mom was one of twelve children who grew up in a rural part of Ireland. When she was a young adult, she immigrated to California and became a dental assistant. There, she met and married my father, who was also an Irish immigrant. Dad was a plastering contractor. He coped with life by drinking. I could always feel the tension in the house rise as it got close to the time Dad was to arrive home from work. Mom would become anxious and agitated, worried that he would stop by the bar, drive home intoxicated, and either harm himself or someone else. She feared they would lose everything.

"Holidays were the hardest because Dad would usually arrive home hours after the planned meal time, and Mom's angst and disappointment were palpable. The drama being played out between them created tremendous stress for my sisters and me, and each of us found our own way to cope with it.

"Growing up, I always felt like I was angry, and Dad was the obvious culprit who inspired the anger, so a number of times I spoke to him about his drinking and the impact it was having on us. Mom seemed to respect my doing that, but when I did it, she would cringe. As I grew into adolescence, I disconnected as much as I could from the home environment and tried to become self-reliant. Sports were great outlets to channel my grief and anger.

"My parents were caring and very practical people, but not affectionate. The fact that we had a roof over our heads, clothes on our backs, and food on the table was proof of their love and commitment to us. Throughout my childhood, I felt a real sadness because I believed I had never been seen for who I was, and because of the lack of nurturing by my parents. I remember as a child craving their attention and affection at times. Then as a teenager, I told myself it didn't matter; that way I supposedly wouldn't be so disappointed. It seemed like Mom always had deep sorrow and looked for solace through her faith. We found out in later years that she had been suffering from undiagnosed depression and anxiety disorder. She was finally put on antidepressants.

"My mom was an avid reader. I remember having stimulating intellectual conversations with her. When I needed advice about relationship issues, I was told to talk to the priest, but I didn't do that because priests didn't get married and what would they know? I, along with Mom's friends and neighbors, would seek her out for her deep wisdom and practical guidance.

"When Mom was in her 70s, her arthritis became debilitating. It impacted her quality of life and she was unable to take long walks. She became housebound. We were brought up Catholic, and Mom believed that suffering with arthritis was a way of doing penance to ensure she would get into Heaven. She refused to see a pain-management specialist. It was really hard to watch her suffering. Over time, Mom's health deteriorated until even practical things became harder for her.

"Two years before Mom's decline, my dad was diagnosed with dementia. Mom did everything for my dad, in spite of her own pain. She would prepare his meals, serve them, and clean up afterwards. We knew it was too much for her, so my older sister Janice and I looked into getting help for our folks. But Mom was not open to help.

"Her steady deterioration and constant pain changed that. Finally, she asked for help and we arranged 24-hour caregiving. She was in such terrible pain.

"Finally, she was hospitalized, and upon discharge, Mom was referred to hospice. I took a leave of absence and stayed with her in California until she died. It was an honor to be there with her. I was her protector. But she wasn't eating or drinking, so it was difficult to watch her change as she grew smaller and dehydrated. Her body held onto life for a while, and eventually, she died.

"I had a sense of her presence very soon after her death. The night she died, I went to pick up my younger sister, Marilyn, to bring her back to my parents' house. My dad drove with me. Not long after we left the house, I felt a warm presence and could sense Mom sitting behind my dad. I heard her say, 'I'm doing well. I'm no longer in pain.'"

The Repair & Reattachment Grief Therapy

When Peggy finished telling me about her mom, I began the Repair & Reattachment Grief Therapy procedure. After the first set of eye movements, she closed her eyes. When she opened them, she said, "My body! The grief is coming up! The grief. I want to squelch it." We did more eye movements and when she opened her eyes, she said, "I want to go to sleep. I have a knot in my stomach. I feel like I want to throw up."

I told her to stay with that feeling and did the eye movements again. This time, the connection began. When Peggy opened her eyes, she said, "I saw Mom. She said, 'I tried to protect you from Dad's drinking, but I see it wasn't the right thing to do. I wish I could have treated you as lovingly when you were growing up as I treated my grandchildren. I can see the importance of that now.'"

I did another set of eye movements and she reported, "I saw my mom. All our pets that had passed on were there jumping up and down and licking Mom's face. In the background, I saw her four sisters who have passed."

After another set of eye movements, Peggy said, "Mom walked away. I said, 'Wait! I want to know if we're doing the right thing with Dad.' She didn't answer me."

I said "Stay with that image," and I did another set of eye movements. She described what she experienced: "Mom's young now, in her 20s or 30s. I saw myself as a child sitting on her lap, but I had adult knowledge. She said to me, 'It's Dad's journey.' Over and over she said that. 'What you do is fine. It is his journey.'"

After more eye movements, Peggy again described what she experienced: "My sisters and Mom were in a circle, and Mom said, 'Do good self-care. I didn't teach you the importance of good self-care.' She started talking about Jake, my dog. Just then, Jake came running in and sat down. Mom said, 'How nice.'"

After more eye movements, Peggy said, "Mom was there again saying, 'Regarding Dad and our life, all those things don't mean anything. I love you. I will always be with you. Dad and your sister Marilyn are being taken care of. Just love her.' Then she showed me we are all connected. Mom said, 'I will always be with you.' They went away happily."

That concluded Peggy's Repair & Reattachment Grief Therapy.

Life Changes from the Repair & Reattachment Grief Therapy

At the end of the session, I asked Peggy to rate again the disturbing memories she had at the beginning of the session on a scale of 0 to 10. She said that all of her disturbing memories had reduced to zeroes.

Several days after the session with Peggy, I received a lovely card with "Thanks" on the outside, written among absolutely beautiful red-orange poppies. On the inside was this message:

Dearest Rochelle,

For all you've done: Blessings to you for creating sacred space for me to connect with my mother! It is a gift I will be forever grateful for receiving.

Much love,
Peggy

Jane, Rebecca's Mom

"It's not about who's got the most. It's about love and connection."

– Rebecca's mother, Jane, in her connection

Rebecca wanted to have a Repair & Reattachment Grief Therapy with her mother, Jane, who died at age 77. "My mom was born in North Dakota in 1910," she said. "Her family immigrated from Russia, but was of German descent. Mom was reared in a strict Baptist home. After she graduated from high school, she went to nursing school in Minneapolis. The school would lock down at night to keep the girls in, but they would sneak out of their windows after hours to party. Mom got caught climbing out of her window at 3:00 a.m. one night, so they kicked her out of school.

"She married Dad when she was 23. They were wild back then, partying a lot. My older brother John was their first child. They had Craig four years later. But they always wanted girls and told my brothers that frequently. Two years after Craig's birth, they finally had a girl, me. Of course, they favored their little girl. They even told Craig they found him in a ditch with rattlesnakes.

"Mom worked with Dad in his grocery store. She had lots of energy and was very outgoing, much more so than Dad. When I was 12, we moved to Los Angeles. Mom got really sick and was in the hospital for two months. Dad lost his business because of all the medical bills.

"Mom bought a tourist store in Venice Beach, California. It was very successful. She had it until she was 70 years old. Mom and Dad worked together at the store. They were really close, doing everything together.

"Then my dad was diagnosed with leukemia, and as he became sicker, he developed shingles. After a long, painful illness, he died in 1984. My mom was totally lost. She had few friends, but she didn't want others to know that, so she put on a great front.

"Mom was on many medications for a variety of medical problems. Her health worried me, but I was in Washington State and she was in California, so I couldn't look in on her. I called Mom one Sunday night and she didn't sound good. I called my brother Craig, who lived in Arizona, and said, "Go check on Mom." He called her and he also thought she didn't sound good.

He wanted to take her to the hospital, but Mom protested that she didn't want to go that night. She said she'd go with him in the morning.

"That night, I had a dream. In the dream my two youngest sons and I were walking Mom down a cliff toward the water. Mom was struggling to walk down the cliff. My sons were urging her on, insisting she could make it. I took off flying down a canyon to the river and awoke. The dream was so unusual I wrote it down in my dream diary, with the time.

"The next morning, Craig called Mom at 7:30 a.m., but there was no answer. He rushed over and walked in to find her dead. I was doing a counseling session when there was a knock on the door, and I was told I had an important call. I picked up the phone, and my brother Craig was on it. He just said, "Mom's dead." I hung up the phone and said to the little girl I was counseling, 'You'll have to excuse me. My mother has died.'

"I flew to California with Mike, the man who later became my second husband. That night, I slept in Mom's bed. I didn't change the sheets. I just wanted to feel her presence. The next day, the lights were going off and on and there were lots of other electrical disturbances. We said, "OK Mom, enough already." My uncle lived in a condo close by and the fountain kept going on and off all night.

"My brothers arranged an open casket funeral. At the end of the funeral, we took a picture of Mom and Dad's nine grandchildren, who hadn't been together for 10 years. When it was developed there was a big orb in the middle of the picture. Mom was a strong personality, and she was going to make her presence known!

"As we were leaving the funeral, the mortician said to me, 'We are closing the casket. Do you want to see her one more time?' My oldest brother said to me, 'You've done so well through the funeral and the service. You didn't even cry once. You're not going back. Let's go.' I really wanted to see her one last time, but relented and we left.

"Mike and I went from the funeral to a beautiful landmark called Bell Rock, that some say has mystical energy. We took trinkets that belonged to Mom and Dad and found a special spot on Bell Rock. We had our own little service and buried the trinkets. Then I said, 'Mom, if you're here, I want some thunder and lightning. Show me a sign.' Instantly, there was a big bolt of lightning and a crack of thunder. Mike and I looked at each other with wide eyes and said, 'Whoa!' After a moment, I collected myself and said, 'Mom, now, I want a rainbow.' But there was no rainbow. So we left.

"As we drove out of the parking lot, Mike looked in his rearview mirror and said, 'Turn around and look.' I did, and there was a huge rainbow that ended right at the spot where we were standing when there was thunder and lightning."

The Repair & Reattachment Grief Therapy

Rebecca finished telling me about her mother, Jane, and we began the Repair & Reattachment Grief Therapy. I asked her what memory was most disturbing for her. She said, "I keep thinking about my brother telling me not to go back to the casket to see Mom one last time. I've regretted that, and it's all because he convinced me to leave."

I did a set of eye movements and Rebecca closed her eyes, focusing on "I've regretted not seeing Mom one last time because he convinced me to leave." When she opened them, she described what she experienced: "I'm really angry at my brother. I'm calling him names. My brother's just sitting down sobbing. I'm seeing him now wanting to be warmer to my other brother and me, and we're not accepting him. I see how insecure he is under a façade of confidence and control, but I am still angry with him. He's such a jerk. I can feel it in my body. I'm trying to find some empathy for him. I have this tug-of-war going on in my head." And at that time, she was sighing and releasing energy. I said to her, "Notice your body and go back inside."

I did several more sets of eye movements and after each, she had another set of images of her brothers. Then, after I did a set of eye movements and she closed her eyes, the connection began. When she opened her eyes, she said, "We were all laughing and saying, 'Let's go see Mom.' I said, 'I think Mom is up at Bell Rock,' and I saw myself running with my brothers up a trail at Bell Rock, laughing. Then I saw Mom. She was standing, looking younger, holding her arms up over her head like a messiah, creating this big rainbow. Then she was scolding all of us. Mom said, 'You all get along. You all get along. Stop being so competitive. It's not about who's got the most. It's about love and connection.'

"Mom said, 'You have a lot to learn about competition. You learned your competitiveness from me. Competitiveness is not a bad thing, but there are nuances you have to learn from it. I will help you. Something very important for you to realize is that we are all here to learn, and there's a lot to learn about. There are three important things to learn about: competitiveness, accomplishment, and not being intimidated by anyone. You are learning these lessons in your career right now. You're doing what you're supposed to be doing. Keep an open mind. Let go of expectations. Be present with what you are doing. It will all come together in a big, ah-ha, ah-ha.'"

We did another set of eye movements. When Rebecca opened her eyes, she said, "I keep seeing Mom walk away with my dad. I want her to stay. I don't want her to go. She says, 'We are always with you. We are always with you.'"

Soon afterward, the session ended.

Kate, Mary's Mom

"I am always with you. Believe! We are all with you."

– Kate, Mary's mom, speaking in her connection

Mary, a regular client of mine, was interested in having a Repair & Reattachment Grief Therapy session with her mother, Kate, who died at age 92. "Mom was a feisty, funny, fearless, driven, smart, unpredictable woman," Mary said. "She would dig in her heels and never give up, especially when it came to getting money. She had people in the palm of her hand. Everyone who knew her was either perplexed with her or loved her.

"Mom was the ultimate strong woman. I felt like a little mouse around her. My uncle even called me 'Minnie Mouse.' I was sort of tiny and gentle and kind, but Mom and my family were outgoing and boisterous. Mom was so overbearing that her manner made me question myself and my worth as a person as early as age three. I always wondered if she really loved me. At times I felt abandoned by her. But in my heart I know Mom loved me.

"Mom always had a hat on, high heels and makeup. She bleached her hair blond when she was about 27 years old. She was a dancer in the Highland Scottish dancing troupe and won many medals.

But Mom wanted to be a singer. She always sang. I remember riding in her yellow Oldsmobile convertible with the top down. If I'd say anything like, 'Isn't this wonderful,' she would burst out with a song like, 'It's wonderful, it's marvelous that you should care for me.'

"I was so quiet, timid, and amused I couldn't get a word in edgewise with Mom. Every time I would say something, she would pick up the words and start belting out a song.

"The best thing I learned from my mom was never give up and don't let anyone take advantage of you. She'd say, 'Mary, look out for number one.' I feel lonely and sad that we weren't closer just before she died.

"Mom died at 92 years of age. When she died I wasn't there. I saw her the day before and tried to talk to her, but she barely had the energy to move because she wasn't drinking and eating. Mom had given up. She was only able to look at me out of the corner of her eye because she was so withered and dehydrated. She died the next day, but I wasn't there.

The Repair & Reattachment Grief Therapy

When Mary finished telling me about her mom, I began the Repair & Reattachment Grief Therapy procedure. I had her focus on the memory that was most distressing to her. She said it was that she wasn't there when her mom died. "I saw her the day before and knew she was dying. I felt so sad that I was not there the next day when she died."

I did a set of eye movements and Mary closed her eyes. When she opened them, she said, "A silly picture just came up. My mom was acting up, sitting on a cloud. I saw my dad with wings like a little cherub. They were smiling and happy. Mom was being hokey and playing games. Dad's heart was always in everything he did, but Mom was always light and silly. It would be just like her to act like that now."

I did another set of eye movements and Mary described what came up. "Dad's mom, Grandma Sophia came up. I just knew it

was her, even though she died before I was born. Then I saw my great grandma on my mother's side. She was very mystical, and the foundation of her family. I felt like they were trying to tell me something."

"OK, focus on that," I said. I did another set of eye movements and Mary closed her eyes. After she opened them, she said, "I saw Grandma Sophia with my dad when he was 5 years old. It looked like my dad. She died at 36 of cancer in the

Grandma Sophia

early 1900s, when my dad was only 10 years old. I never met her, of course, but that was her. She was 5 foot 11 and very sophisticated looking in her pictures."

I did another set of eye movements. "I felt so guilty," Mary said. "Heartbroken. My mom must have felt so abandoned. I want her to forgive me."

I said, "Ask her." After another set of eye movements, Mary reported, "I asked Mom to forgive me. She said, 'So, what are you gonna give me?' That's just like her. So I gave her a big hug. I said, 'I love you Mom.'" Mary smiled and paused for a moment, then said, "Rochelle, a couple of months after she died, I felt her hand touching my face. Do you think that really was her?"

I said, "Well, ask her the question." So, we did another set of eye movements and Mary closed her eyes. When she opened them, she said, "I asked her, 'Was that your hand touching my face after you died when I was lying in my bed?' Mom said, 'I am always with you. Believe. We are all with you.'"

We did more sets of eye movements and Mary was getting messages about what she would do with her life. "Something is spurring me on to bring justice to an unjust world," she said at one point. When she opened her eyes after another set of eye movements, she said, "What came up was my great-grandma who helped start the Salvation Army in Scotland. And I was hearing Saint Francis of Assisi's words, 'Where there is sadness, bring joy. Where there is despair, bring hope.' It kind of went on and on, like they're telling me not to be so self-absorbed and concerned about my financial situation and everything else in my life. I should help out the world. I should get out there and do something. That's what they were saying."

After another set of eye movements, Mary said, "I got the image of a huge hotel my grandmother's family had built. Now, it's turned into senior housing. It started out to make a profit, but now it's become shelter for people who need it. It is helping people now, even though it started as a profit-making venture. That's where my life is heading."

With that, the session ended.

Life Changes from the Repair & Reattachment Grief Therapy

When Mary began her session, the memory with the highest disturbance score was "When she died I wasn't there." It was a 10 plus, plus, plus. By the end of the session, her rating for that memory had reduced to a 1.

Just before she left, Mary described the change in her life direction she felt was happening: "I need to sit quietly and do some critical thinking and some spiritual thinking. That's how I'm going to get answers to my questions. They're heading me in that direction."

When Mary came back for a second session, I asked her, "How have you been doing?" She said, "I feel like my mom is always around now. Something amazing happened. A day after I met with you, my daughter Elizabeth and I got into the car and immediately Elizabeth said, 'I smell a rose. It's like Grandma's perfume, like Windsong and Rose.' Mom used to wear both. I know she was there."

Wiley, Maggie's Brother

"*Turn away from the dense, dark, and gray. Look outside. See the sun, the rainbow, the source.*"

– Maggie's brother, Wiley, in her connection

Maggie works as a hospice nurse and has a master's degree in social work. She wanted to connect with her brother, who died at age 59, so she made an appointment and came to my office. After she put on the audio bilateral headset and was comfortable, she began describing her brother, Wiley.

"Wiley was the eldest child of the four of us. Because of the 11-year age difference between us, we were not very close when I was a child. When I was 8 years old, Wiley left for college, and after graduation he moved out of state to pursue a career as an elementary physical-education teacher. When he was in his 30s, he became a paramedic. Wiley loved being a paramedic. He loved the uniform and the brotherhood of firefighters.

"Wiley settled in Arizona with his wife Miriam and had three sons. In 1989, I moved to Arizona with my husband and daughter and was able to establish a close relationship with my brother and his sons.

"A few years later, I moved back to our home state, California. Soon afterward, our father died. Within a year, Wiley experienced a life-threatening illness that really shook him up, forcing him to address his own mortality. Not long after, our mother died suddenly in her sleep. This seemed to unmoor him, and he reached out to me in ways he had never done before. Through our grief, we became closer. When things were difficult, I would call him, asking him if he was still there, and he would answer, "Yes, Maggie, I'm still here." That was a great comfort to me.

"Before his death, Wiley had made plans to retire and return to California to be closer to us. I was counting on having more time with him. My grief for him is not just for loss of the relationship we had, but also for the future we were never able to share.

"The January before Wiley's death, he developed a swollen ankle and believed it to be a simple strain. He didn't follow up on his doctor's request to have an ultrasound to rule out a blood clot. Three weeks later, he became short of breath and went to the same doctor, but the doctor didn't remember the swollen ankle, so he misdiagnosed him. The night before Wiley died, he emailed me to say the doctor told him he had pneumonia. He said he didn't believe it; he had never had pneumonia before. I kidded him in the email, hiding my concern. I had a fleeting thought that I should call him, but didn't.

"Wiley took a nap the next day and never woke up. He experienced a massive blood clot in his lungs that ended his life. I regret that I didn't call him. It causes me great sadness to think I may have been able to direct Wiley to the kind of medical care that could have saved his life.

"Three days later I had a dream. An elf-like young male spirit woke me and said to me, 'Wiley's on the phone. He wants to tell you he's alive.' I got on the phone and said to him, 'What are you Lazarus or something?' He laughed and said, 'Yes, I am still alive.' And then Wiley said 'Thank you for pushing me to get after stuff.' I sensed that he was standing in front of me holding a phone, and just behind him, my parents were standing. I said something about our sister Joyce and he directed me to let our family priest help her. Then the phone went dead and I heard many different phones all over the house start ringing. That's when I woke up.

"As an Irish piper played, we spread his ashes in the bay in front of Mom and Dad's beach place, the same waters into which we had released our father's ashes ten years before. It was exactly as Wiley had requested."

That was the end of Maggie's story about her brother Wiley.

The Repair & Reattachment Grief Therapy

It was a beautiful day, so we took a 10- minute break and she walked around the building. When she came back, we started the Repair & Reattachment Grief Therapy procedure, focusing on her most distressing memory, which she rated a 10 plus, plus. It was that she didn't call Wiley when he emailed her that he was being treated for pneumonia. She emailed him back, but didn't call. He died the next day.

I guided her through a set of eye movements and she closed her eyes. When she opened them, she said, "I saw myself on the computer emailing Wiley. I know I should call him but I don't. It wouldn't have made a difference. The decision was already made. It was out of my control."

After another set of eye movements, she closed her eyes and the connection began. When she opened her eyes, she said, "My grandmother came to me. She was reassuring me: 'Let it go, let it go.'"

I guided her through another set of eye movements. When Maggie opened her eyes, she said "I was feeling soft and quiet, looking at a white, empty place, like the inside of a cloud. It felt like a meeting place, and they were all there. I saw Mom. She wanted to comfort me by pointing out the emanating rays of the sun. I put my face toward the light to energize myself. 'It's so beautiful,' Mom said. 'There's power from the source right there.'"

After another set of eye movements, Maggie said, "I was in a white, open area, like a waiting area. Mom came to me and showed me times we had together in the Mill Street home when I was a child. She was playing the piano and I was sitting on the floor listening, just the two of us. Mom is happy and I feel loved. Then we're on the couch and she is reading to me. I lean into her arms and see a rapid review of images from my childhood when Mom comforted me: treating skinned knees, caring for me when I was sick, and making lunches for me. I saw her tears when she was on the phone learning that her dad had died. Then she was holding me for comfort."

I did another set of eye movements. "I'm being shown her father's funeral," Maggie continued. "I can see Mom sitting at the gravesite while my grandmother comforts me. I get the messages 'strength,' 'love,' and 'comfort.'"

After another set of eye movements, Maggie said, "I'm in the waiting room again, and my grandmother appears, smiling and happy. She's showing me images of our time together. Grandmother's teaching me to knit." Maggie smiled. "Then I saw her unraveling my knitting—what a perfectionist! I saw all the dresses and the afghans she made. She was so strong. I was tapping into my mother's generation and all the women before me, all that they faced. Even the hard things I face are OK. I'm just the next generation. I am one of them. And then I heard, 'You are not alone.' They're seeing how hard I work."

I did another set of eye movements. When Maggie opened her eyes, she said, "They're showing me the image of Eleanor, my daughter, who's living. Her body opens up and the light of her soul is revealed; it is beautiful, exquisite. They're telling me she's the next generation. They know that I get it. Grandmother showed me a tapestry. It is the tapestry of our lives."

I guided her through another set of eye movements and she said, "Now I'm seeing Grandmother riding in a car with Wiley and he's teasing her. She loved that. She's got one hand on Wiley's shoulder and one hand on mine. There's power and stability in the relationship between Grandmother, Wiley, and me. Our connection to her is the same somehow.

"Then Grandmother said to me, 'Wiley is still healing his feelings. He's tired, but it was all decided beforehand. I am helping him heal. I have it covered, Maggie. Hand it over to me.' Wiley's happy. He's laughing, teasing, and still telling jokes."

After another set of eye movements, Maggie reported, "He's not hurting anymore. The pain has been left behind. And then the words came up, 'Time and patience.' I heard Wiley say, 'Think about my boys. I'm very happy you're involved with my boys. Thank you, thank you.' He's trying to make me laugh. 'OK, Wiley, you're very funny,' I said. He said, 'Yes, we're all funny. Laugh, Maggie.'"

I did another set of eye movements. When she opened her eyes, she said, "We were all laughing. Mom was pointing at the sun. Wiley was showing me the same light source Mom did, saying, 'Open up to it, lean into it. It's there. The light and rainbow are one and the same. It's outside your window every day. Turn your body away from the dense stuff, the dark and the gray.' I have the feeling he meant the family issues between my sisters and me that I can't fix. Dad put himself between the dense, dark stuff and me. Wiley said, 'Look out the window and see the sun, the rainbow, the source. Look away from the dense stuff.' Then I saw my daughter Eleanor with a blue light and son Patrick with a red light. Both were beautiful lights, revealing their souls."

I guided her through another set of eye movements. When Maggie opened her eyes, she said, "The sun was on my face. I was in the sunlight. I was flying toward the source. They were reminding me, 'It's OK.' Then I got a hug from everybody one at a time. I held my brother really hard. They love me so much, and they know I miss them all. They gave me some tools and said, 'Hold onto these. They're light. You'll be able to use these. Turn away from the dark. We'll see you in your dreams.' I hugged Wiley, squeezed him, and cried on his shoulder. Rochelle, I feel comforted and loved. I am not alone."

Life Changes from the Repair & Reattachment Grief Therapy

We started the Repair & Reattachment Grief Therapy procedure focusing on Maggie's most distressing memory, which she rated a 10 plus, plus. It was the memory that she didn't call Wiley when he emailed her. After the session, I said "Bring up the memory and on the scale of 0 to 10, where is it now?" She said, "It doesn't register." I asked, "It doesn't register?" She said emphatically, "It doesn't register! It doesn't even register!"

Larry, Lori's Husband

"It literally, literally changed my memory."

– Lori, about her connection with her husband, Larry

"I don't want to get married. Let's just hang out together," Lori said to Larry when they were dating. The words apparently had no effect. They had 26 wonderful years of marriage. I did a Repair & Reattachment Grief Therapy session with Lori on the fifth anniversary of Larry's death. "We were married in the mountains at sunset," Lori said. "He really was my Prince Charming. People would say to us all the time, 'We've never seen a marriage like yours.' We had two beautiful children, Lana and Lucas.

"'I'm going to die young,' he often said. 'Men in our family don't live long. If something ever happens to me, go to the black box.' I knew the black box was among his things, but I didn't know what was in it.

"On the day Larry died, I had asked him to cut down an old pampas grass bush with a chainsaw. He worked all day long and wasn't happy about it. That was unusual for him. That evening, we went to see a movie and got home about 11:30. I went down to the basement to get on the computer. I heard Larry in the kitchen, so I figured he was getting something to eat and would come down in a minute to play Party Poker on the computer as he often did.

"After a while, he hadn't come down, so I went upstairs to see what he was doing. He was in the bedroom, sitting up in bed with the TV on. His eyes were open, so I said, "What are you watching?" He didn't respond. I asked again, "What are you watching?" and he still didn't respond. I got close and looked in his eyes. They were staring straight ahead, and he wasn't moving.

"I started screaming, 'Don't you dare do this to me,' and grabbed the phone. I called 911. They told me what to do. I frantically pounded on Larry's chest. He was still warm under the covers but his chest started getting cold. Then I heard the 'death rattle' coming from Larry. I reached down and did mouth-to-mouth resuscitation on him. But the more air I blew in, the louder the rattle became. After a few minutes, the emergency team arrived. I thought, "The professionals are here. They can do anything." The emergency team worked on him, but it was too late. He was gone.

"The next day, after all the funeral arrangements were done, I found the black box Larry wanted me to open if he died. In it was an envelope with five love letters he sent to me when I was in college. But there was another envelope that had written on it, 'In case of an accident open this letter.' I opened the envelope, unfolded this letter, and read it:

Dearest Lori,

> We'll sing in the Sunshine
> We'll laugh every day
> We'll sing in the Sunshine
> and be on our way

When you read this please remember the good times. The fun, the trips, raising our wonderful kids. I love you more than anything in the world and I always will be watching over you. You made my life worth living. Smile when you think of the 'hoot.' Don't cry. Remember—don't grieve. Let Lana and Lucas know how much I loved them and tell them to be good to people and good things will happen.

I lived life feeling I was lucky. Reality was never my strong suit. Thinking of magic was a lot more enjoyable. I was lucky to have a beautiful sexy wife. I was lucky to support my family. I was lucky to have 2 great kids. I was lucky, lucky, lucky.

> We had fun, love, excitement
> and sky rockets and stars

Love always,
Larry "The Polish Hawaiian"

I asked her how sad reading the letter was for her. She said, "Very sad."

Then she described something odd. "You know, Rochelle, a strange thing happens now. Lucas and Lana are both living out of state. When one of them comes home, as they're entering the driveway, the outside lights start blinking on and off. But it happens only the first day they come home. I often wonder if that's Larry."

The Repair & Reattachment Grief Therapy

Lori said she had finished her story, so we were ready to begin the Repair & Reattachment Grief Therapy. She said, "Can I ask Larry for advice about what I should do with our son, Luke?" I said, "We'll just have to let whatever happens happen. We don't know if he'll be able to give you an answer to that question." I said that to her because we can't guarantee anything in a Repair & Reattachment Grief Therapy. We're not in charge. The loved ones involved in the connection are in control all the way through.

We decided the most disturbing memories were when Lori was pounding on Larry's chest trying to revive him and when she read the letter to her that was in the black box. I did a set of eye movements and Lori closed her eyes. The connection began immediately. When she opened them, she said, "I got a message from Larry. He said, 'I love you. If you are alone and sad, call my name, "Larry, Larry, Larry" or do the puzzle picture of me.' I have a jigsaw puzzle that is a picture of Larry when it's put together. Then he said to me, 'I like to come to you when you're happy and smiling. I'll visit in dreams.'"

I did another set of eye movements. When Lori opened her eyes, she said, "Larry was telling me about our son, Luke. I've been worried about him. Larry said, 'Luke will be Luke. Let him alone. Let Luke be Luke.' And then he said, 'Yes, we do the outside strobe lights when the kids come home the first day.'" He must have been listening in on our conversation."

Lori said to me, "I really miss his warm hugs. I miss them so much." I did another set of eye movements and she closed her eyes. Within just a few seconds, with her eyes closed, she said, "Ooh, I feel this warmth, a very warm pulsating feeling in my forehead, in my hands, in my legs. I feel hot all over." I knew it was Larry hugging her.

Lori opened her eyes and told me, "Larry said, 'You need to guide yourself. Grab every joy there is available, my sweet. You will be coming to me again someday. I saw you upset. I was with you when you walked up the stairs and I was gone.'"

I did another set of eye movements, and when Lori opened her eyes, she continued: "He said, 'I have to go. The best thing you can do for me is to be happy. Don't listen to anyone, even the children. You don't need me for decisions, but I will be there. When your time here is over, you betcha we'll be together.' Then everything went to a whirl of fuzz and dark and then black."

The connection had ended. Lori said, "He's watching me. I got to talk to him when he was watching me. It literally, literally changed my memory." The memories of Larry's passing, with sadness, loss, and never being able to connect again had changed to these new memories of connection and overwhelming love.

Life Changes from the Repair & Reattachment Grief Therapy

At the beginning of the session, she had rated three memories as 10, very disturbing: pounding on Larry's chest to try to revive him, reading the letter he wrote to her that was in the black box, and realizing he was dying or dead as he was sitting up in bed. I asked her to rate them for disturbance at the end of the session. She rated them all as zeroes, meaning no disturbance.

The next day, Lori came to my office, and as she entered said excitedly, "I know what I'm gonna do!" I said, "Well, sit down and tell me." She said, "Well, I can but I know what I'm gonna do." I said, "OK, what are you gonna do?" She finally sat down.

"I'm going to travel the world. I'm going to sell that big house I've been taking care of, where I've had to be the master gardener and I've had to wallpaper it and keep it up. I've taken care of that house for four years since Larry passed away. I'm putting that house up for sale and I'm leaving. I'm going to travel the world. I'm going to go visit some relatives first, and then I'm going to go to Costa Rica and France. And when I come back I plan to build a house on the 30 acres we have on that lake in Minnesota and that's where I'll live."

I said, "Well, do you want to put the headset on and do a session about it?" She immediately replied, "Nope, I don't need to. I know what I'm gonna do. I really don't even have to be here because I know what I'm gonna do." We had a pleasant talk about her plans and she left energetic and beaming.

A month later, I received this letter from Lori:

> *Dear Rochelle, I have been saying my Larry was the trunk of our tree and when he died the branches all fell to the ground.*
>
> *The children looked to me to hold them high in the air, firmly through the winds and to the sun. I could not.*
>
> *When the trunk disappeared my branch, the heaviest, fell hard unto and into the ground.*
>
> *And Rochelle, like a mole, you dug a tunnel from the root of the great trunk to the part of me that had fallen hardest and had not seen the sun.*
>
> *The nutrients that had been denied the branch pulsed through and stood me up again. Upright as a sapling with bark from a mature tree.*
>
> *I see the sun and can feel the breezes once more. I have a knowing my new leaves will dance and give nutrients to my new roots.*
>
> *Thank you.*
>
> *Lori*

Lois, Terry's Mom

"It's not your fault. Don't feel guilty. I'm all right."

– Lois, Terry's mom, in her connection with Terry

Terry's mother, Lois, passed away three years before Terry came to see me. Her mom was in her 80s when she died.

"My mom was really a strong-willed person," Terry said. "She raised my sister and me by herself. I was the bad child in the family. I hung out with people I shouldn't have, mostly military guys older than me. That made her angry. I was 18 when Mom married her third husband and moved to his house. Bill, my boyfriend, moved into the house with me so I wouldn't be alone. He didn't mind, and Mom didn't care because she was doing her own thing. After we were married, Mom didn't feel comfortable around Bill because of his personality and the way he treated our kids, so during those years when Mom and I lived apart, we didn't communicate much.

"I had my own problems with Bill, and after many years, we divorced. Mom and I grew closer after that. Soon I met Richard and we married. Mom really liked Richard and became close to him. Those years were very different from my earlier years with Mom. My time with her and our talks became wonderful memories for me. She loved people, especially the grandkids, and was always supportive.

"Then, when she was in her 80s, Mom got Parkinson's disease. I moved in with her to take care of her. I became her best friend, and she was my best friend and companion. I would regularly drive her in her Cadillac to the beauty salon to get her nails and hair done. I would park and she would get out and go in.

"Then, the last time we went to the beauty salon, my mom got out of the car as she always had done, and as she walked up to go inside, she fell hard onto the concrete. The image of her falling became imprinted in my mind. I see it all the time now. The worst part of seeing it over and over is that I knew she was falling but I wasn't close enough to help her.

"I ran over to her and could see that it was a bad fall. I was really scared. I held her hand waiting for the ambulance to arrive. The ambulance came and they put her in. I went home to get the insurance cards, then drove to the hospital in a daze. I ran into the emergency ward and found her. I talked to her and she was able to talk to me, but it was the last time I would talk to her. She just said, "Terry, I want to hold your hand." When they examined her, they said 'We think she's had an aneurism. If she has, she's not going to make it.'

"That hospital didn't have a trauma unit to take care of an aneurism, so they had to transport her to another hospital. They put her into another ambulance and I drove behind them to the other hospital. When I got there, I found out that during the long trip, she was vomiting and it was getting into her lungs. They had to resuscitate her on the way.

"They put her into the intensive care unit on a respirator with a tube in her mouth. She couldn't talk, so the only communication I had was looking into her eyes when I talked to her. I could see that she was suffering terrible pain. Her arm was damaged and needed surgery, but they couldn't operate until she was out of intensive care. For three weeks, we all just lived there.

"Finally, the doctor met with us and said Mom suffered brain damage from the fall. We could either turn off the respirator and let her go or let her live on the respirator. We decided to take her off the respirator. As we stood by her bed, they turned off the respirator. She breathed on her own. So they took her by ambulance to hospice.

"I walked with her as they wheeled her into her room. She had a very frightened look on her face. Two days later, we knew the end was near. She still couldn't talk, so we communicated with her through her eyes. I said goodbye to her.

"We thought she would be OK for a while, so when my Mom's sister, Aunt Jean, came, I went to work and my sister went to have a shower. I know Mom was waiting for Aunt Jean to come. While we were gone and Aunt Jean was there, Mom took her last breath. They cleaned her up, took all of the tubes out, laid a pretty blanket over her, and put flowers in her hands. They toasted a sendoff to her with sparkling cider."

The Repair & Reattachment Grief Therapy

When Terry finished telling me the story, I began the Repair & Reattachment Grief Therapy procedure. The most distressing memory was the image of her mom falling on the concrete. I guided her through ten minutes of repeated cycles of eye movements and experiences with her eyes closed. Then, when she opened her eyes after a set of eye movements, she said, "Mom came to me. She said, 'It's not your fault. Don't feel guilty. I'm all right.'"

We had to end the session shortly after that.

Terry's Second Session

Terry came in for the second session looking very sad. She said, "The anniversary of my mom's death was this month. You know, there are weird noises in the house. The phone rings and when we pick it up, no one is on the line. Then, one day, the doorbell rang repeatedly, but when we went to the door, no one was there." I said, "Well, let's see what's going on." Terry put on the earphones and we began the Repair & Reattachment Grief Therapy procedure.

I did a set of eye movements while she focused on the

Richard

question, "Is that you, Mom? Are you making weird things happen in the house?" She closed her eyes. When she opened them, she said, "Right away, 'Yes' came up. They are doing it. It's either my mom or Richard, my deceased husband. He's been gone ten years."

I said, "Focus on the doorbell ringing when there's no one there. Ask whether they're doing that." I did a set of eye movements and she closed her eyes. When she opened them, she said, "I think it was a 'Yes,' so then I asked, 'Why didn't it happen the day before when everybody was there for my birthday party?' I knew it was Richard who answered. He said, 'I wanted to make contact at your birthday party, but there was too much going on. I waited until it was quiet. I could come the day after your birthday party because Mother and you were there alone. I did it for you because you are the believers. I wanted you to know I was there. Believe!'"

I did another set of eye movements. When she opened her eyes, she said, "I got the words 'Be patient. Get happy.' I think it's coming from both my mom and Richard."

I did several more sets of eye movements, and after each set she described the words of encouragement she was getting: "Don't be sad. Be happy. Be content. Live your life. You can do it. Like yourself. Be a whole person. Work hard. Help others."

I said, "Ask if there's anything more that your mother has to say to you." I did a set of the eye movements and she closed her eyes. When she opened them, she said she heard, "Live your own life. Have faith. Just be yourself."

Then I said, "Ask Richard if there's anything he wants to say before we stop." I did another set of eye movements and she reported that Richard told her, "Be happy. Live for yourself." With that, we knew the connection had ended.

I closed the file and stood up. As I did, I noticed that the power on my CD player was off. I never turn it off during the entire time I'm in the office. I press the "Stop" button to stop the CD when a session is done, but I always leave the player on.

I asked Terry, "Did you turn that power button off?" She said, "No." I said, "Well, I didn't turn it off. Did you see me turn it off?" She said, "No, you didn't turn it off." I thought, "Oh my gosh. They were letting us know, and putting an exclamation point on it, that they were here today."

The doorbell ringing, weird noises in the house, the phone ringing, and this CD player turning off were all related. There are ways that they can and do communicate. They come to let us know they're always around.

Life Changes from the Repair & Reattachment Grief Therapy

At the beginning of the session, Terry had several memories she said were highly disturbing, with ratings of 10. They were memories of her mom falling on the concrete, hearing that if there was an aneurism, she wasn't going to make it, being in the hospital for three weeks not knowing what would happen, taking her mom off the respirator, her mom dying, the funeral, and the graveside ceremony.

When I asked her to rate the level of disturbance when she thought of these memories following the connection, all of the disturbing memories had reduced to 0.

Joe, Christine's Husband

"He kissed me! He hugged me! We were holding each other!"

– Christine, after connecting with her husband, Joe

Christine sat solemnly in my office, drained from a year of grieving for her husband, Joe, who passed away on the day after Christmas 2009. "He was a wonderful man," she said. "He loved me. He understood me and protected me and cared for me. I can still hear his laugh. We'd laugh over silly things like a monkey on TV. He would say, 'That's you' and I would say, 'No, that's you.' The family meant everything to him, and he worked very hard to provide for us. He was a wonderful husband and father.

"Joe loved to travel, so our family was always going on vacations and exploring new places. We loved walking on beaches looking for shells. We did everything together. We had a Christmas tree farm and worked side by side  every day. We'd stay at the cabin on the tree farm making wreaths together. The cabin was precious to Joe and me.

"Joe had polio at age 3 that affected his body for the rest of his life. He worked as hard and as long as he was able, but had terrible pain in his legs. It got worse, and eventually he was unable to keep working. Joe resisted going on disability because working meant so much to him, and he was very proud of what he could do. But finally, the pain was just too much to bear, and he reluctantly went on disability. It was a traumatic time for Joe.

"We retired to our precious cabin, where we felt safe. After a short time, Joe began to say that his body felt really strange. We didn't know it then, but a cancer was growing inside him. He became increasingly nauseated and would throw up everything he ate. We went to different doctors for a month, but they couldn't figure out what was wrong. Finally, they gave him a CAT scan and found lesions on his liver.

"Then he had hiccups for ten days, so they did more tests. The biopsy showed he had bile duct cancer. We were both in shock. The miserable time that followed was an ongoing battle for Joe.

But we said confidently, 'We'll beat this bile duct cancer' and had every hope we could.

"He started chemo and the cancer shrank some, but we felt the doctor wasn't giving his all, so we went to the Cancer Wellness Center. Then we went to Fred Hutchinson Research, and to Cancer Care Alliance, and then back to the Cancer Wellness Center. They all gave him treatments and we tried them all, including a huge cocktail with a platinum drug and vitamin C infusions. At times he felt better for a month or two, but it didn't last.

"We went to a healing place in Sedona. They did stem-cell therapy, vitamin C infusions, and whole-body hyperthermia, and other treatments. We saw doctors in Germany for treatment and massage therapy, still feeling optimistic and staying upbeat. When we returned home from Germany, a CAT scan showed the tumor had grown and closed off his bile ducts even more.

"We continued to live with hope and persisted in trying to find the right help. We went to the Swedish Hospital, but they wanted to do chemo; Joe had been through so much of it that he didn't want anymore. So we tried natural treatments. I found a clinic in Tijuana, Mexico, that did a different kind of therapy called light therapy, so we went there. But they were really disorganized, and the conventional medicine they gave him didn't work.

"Joe went downhill after that, really fast. One night, he didn't feel well at 4 a.m. one morning, so I called 911 and they transported him to the hospital. A CAT scan showed that the tumors had grown. The emergency room doctor just said to Joe, 'The cancer is getting the best of you. You should go to hospice.' So we did. There, Joe's doctor told me he may live one week.

"One week. We were still hopeful. Joe didn't want to die. He was full of life and didn't want to stay at hospice. He kept saying, 'Get me out of here.' I was trying everything and I still had a lot of hope.

"They put a catheter in him to drip 24-hour pain medication. Joe's body was shutting down, but I couldn't give up. I was feeding him and I was there with him, still hopeful.

"Then one night, his breathing changed. I gave him water and did whatever I could to make him comfortable, but each hour his breathing changed. At 5:09 in the morning, with his brother beside him and me holding him, he closed his eyes partway and took his last breath. No words were spoken. I couldn't believe what was happening. It was like the light went out in both of us. I was empty, completely empty. My heart was breaking in a million pieces. I couldn't stop crying.

"The next week we had the memorial. I went to him, stood beside him, and put items on him, special items. At the end of the memorial, I looked at him for the last time, and we buried him.

"I went to our cabin alone."

The Repair & Reattachment Grief Therapy

Christine had finished telling me about Joe. After a break, we settled in to begin the Repair & Reattachment Grief Therapy. I asked her about her sadness when she brought up each of the memories she described. On the scale of 0 to 10, there were lots of 10s, 10 pluses, and 10 plus, pluses. But there was one 10 plus, plus, plus: the memory of the night he died when, as she held him, he took his last breath.

I told Christine to think of that and the image or picture that went with it, and I guided her through the eye movements. She closed her eyes. After a short time, she opened them and described what she experienced. "Darkness. It's unclear. There's a light. I saw light and then nothing." I followed with more sets of eye movements and she continued to describe colors, swirls, and lights, but the connection wasn't happening. I checked on the sadness associated with the image of Joe's dying. "Where is it now," I asked. "It's a 10 plus, plus." It had reduced by only a "plus." Normally, after repeated bilateral stimulation, the sadness would reduce quite a bit. So I went back to it.

"OK, bring up the images again," and I did several more sets of eye movements, followed by her closing her eyes to process the experiences. But she still described nothing beyond vague images. I asked her again, "Where is the sadness with that image now?" She said, "A 10 plus." It had reduced by only a "plus." I asked her, "What is the worst part of that memory?" Christine said, "Death wasn't an option." Then I knew that something associated with that was holding her back. I said, "Stay with that thought, 'Death wasn't an option,' and watch my fingers."

I guided Christine through more eye movements and she experienced more lights and patterns, but no connection. Whatever was blocking her wasn't coming out yet. I asked, "So what is it now that's bothering you about that memory?" She responded, "The horror of it. The devastation and failure." That was getting closer to whatever was affecting her so deeply it was blocking the connection.

I told Christine to keep that in mind and did another set of eye movements. When she opened her eyes, she said, "I saw the yellow gown they put on him. The room was spinning. I'm spinning right now. This room is spinning. I'm feeling dizziness, unpleasantness, nausea." Whatever was bothering her was affecting her physically as it came closer to the surface.

I did another set of eye movements. Christine opened her eyes and said, "It went blank, and then I got that it was my fault. I failed. I tried to keep him alive for both of us, right up to the last hours in hospice. I wanted a miracle, and I was going to go anywhere to find it. It was my responsibility. I feel guilty because I failed."

That was what had been blocking the connection: her deeply felt guilt and feeling of failure. It was so consuming that she couldn't get past those emotions to relax and let the connection unfold naturally. So, I stopped for a moment and said, "Christine, all the doctors and researchers at Harvard Medical Center, Cancer Care Alliance, the Mayo Clinic, UCLA Medical Center, and every other cancer-research center in the world are looking for a cure but haven't found it. They can't fix it. Do you think you could do that when they can't?" She looked at me and smiled weakly, shaking her head.

We targeted "It was my responsibility. I feel guilty because I failed." I guided Christine through a set of eye movements and she closed her eyes. When she opened them, she said, "I saw the grave and the color green. Then it just released. All the dizziness, all the nausea and head spinning. It just released." The feeling of guilt and failure she uncovered was released from her body. The connection soon began.

I did another set of eye movements and Christine closed her eyes. After a few seconds, she opened them. "Oh, this is really strange. There was a mountainous outcropping of rock peaks. A white light came down and a person in a spacesuit appeared. He took off his helmet and had a head of black hair like Joe's. Then I felt a cold sensation around my mouth. He kissed me!" She smiled broadly.

I said, "Ask the question, 'Was that you, Joe, and did you kiss me?'" I did the eye movements, and after a short time Christine opened her eyes. "Right away I got 'Yes!' Then there was cold all over me, up and down my arms like we were hugging and holding each other."

When it appeared the connection was ending, I said to her, "Is there anything you want to say to Joe before he leaves?" She said, "Yes. I want to say 'I love you.'" I told her, "Go ahead and say that. Follow my fingers and think those words." I guided her through the eye movements and she closed her eyes. Christine sat quietly with tears running down her cheeks. With her eyes still closed, she said, "He's telling me he loves me too." After a few more seconds, Christine said, "Now he's fading away."

I said, "Ask if there's anything he wants to say before we close and he fades completely." When Christine opened her eyes, she said, "I got from him, 'I'll be back.'"

With that, the session ended.

Life Changes from the Repair & Reattachment Grief Therapy

I spoke with Christine on the phone two days after the session. She said, "The funniest thing happened yesterday. All of a sudden, about 24 hours after my connection with you, I just felt like my spirit lifted. Something really changed. I felt like a big weight came off of me. I wonder what that was about." I said, "Don't go into the left brain, your logical mind, just notice that something wonderful happened and say, 'Thank you.'"

Christine's Second Session

When Christine came in for her second session a week after the first, she started speaking almost before she had sat down. "Rochelle, I remembered something that happened before our first session. I was meditating and had a meditation dream. Joe spoke to me. He said 'Listen to "Rocket Man" by Elton John.' I had forgotten that. So last week I got a recording of the song and there's a line in it that says, "I miss the earth so much, I miss my wife." It's an astronaut, a rocket man, singing. That's why Joe came to me in the connection in a space suit!" We were both amazed at the connection between her meditation dream and the perceived connection.

"I am learning to accept what happened," Christine said. "I talk to him every day. My time is not so weepy. I am more into acceptance."

After that, we began a brief Repair & Reattachment Grief Therapy session. We decided to target his saying, "I'll be back." I guided Christine through a set of eye movements, and she closed her eyes. When she opened them, she said, "Joe came right away. He took me back to the outcropping of rocks. We were just standing there looking up at a mountain, and he gave me a KISS again! I felt a tickle on my nose. I said, 'Is that you tickling my nose?' He said, 'Yes,' and then he blew on my left eye. He had his hand on my forehead, like this (Christine put her hand on her forehead) and his other hand on my neck, like he was holding me. Then he stopped holding my head and neck and we got up. We walked in the grassy field together, in front of the mountain. My nose started tickling as we were walking. There was a butterfly on my nose. Joe went to push it away and it fluttered around us."

I said, "Ask him, 'Is there anything you want to say, Joe, before we close today?'" I did a set of eye movements and when Christine opened her eyes, she said, "I asked him, and he said "I LOVE you! I MISS you! He also said the book you're writing about these connections will be 'fantastic.'"

I said, "Ask him if you should be part of my presentation at the upcoming conference." I guided her through a set of eye movements, and when she opened her eyes, she said, "He told me, 'Yes.' Then he said, 'Remember, we can visit like this in dreams. I am around you a lot. When you feel a tickle, it's me.'"

With that, the session ended.

Life Changes from the Repair & Reattachment Grief Therapy

Two days later, Christine called and told me that on her way home after the session, she had a joyous feeling and the words came to her, "This was the MOST PROFOUND experience of MY LIFE!"

At the beginning of the session, Christine rated the disturbance of lots of memories at 10s, 10 plusses, 10 plus, plusses, and one 10 plus, plus, plus: when he took his last breath, with his brother on one side and her on the other side holding him. At the end of the session, Christine said that all of the disturbances from the memories had reduced to zeroes.

Christine, Kay's Daughter

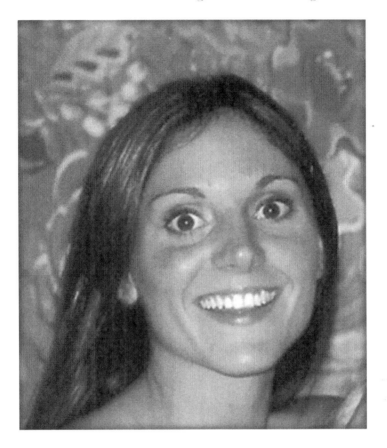

"I love you Mom, and I'm right here with you."

– Christine, Kay's daughter, in her connection

Kay's daughter, Christine, was 27 when she was killed in a car accident. "Christine was a free spirit," Kay said. "She was going to college on her own seven-year plan. She would go to school, stop and travel, then go back to school until the travel urge got her again. I'd say, 'You really need to get a job,' and she'd say, 'I know, I know.'

"When she was home, she liked spending time with us, especially going out to dinner with her dad and me. Christine always included us in what she did. She even had us go hear her

boyfriend's band play. She would say to her boyfriend, 'If you don't like hanging out with my parents, we're just not gonna make it.'

"One evening, we were going to attend a concert and stay overnight in the city where she was living. She wanted us to come by the restaurant where she worked before we went to the concert. I told her we would try, but we ran out of time and didn't stop by. After the concert, I left her a voicemail to come by our hotel and she called me back, but we were in a noisy restaurant, so I didn't hear the phone ring.

"The next day, I called her, but we just kept playing telephone tag. Then the day after that, she left me a message on my voicemail at my work to call her. I listened to the message between meetings, but it was a crazy, crazy day at work and I forgot to call her back until 9:00 that night. She wasn't there, so I left her a voicemail. The next day, I left another voicemail. We always talked every other day, if not every day, but during this time, I didn't talk to her for a week.

"Then, at the end of the week, at 3:00 in the morning, she was driving her boyfriend home from the place his band was playing. She took a hairpin turn too fast, lost control of the car, and hit a tree. The crash severed her carotid artery and she lost a lot of blood.

"They finally got ahold of me at 7:30 in the morning at work. She was in surgery when they called. Her brother picked me up at work and we drove up to the hospital. She came out of surgery at 9 a.m. They said she had a stroke on the right side of the brain. When we got to the Trauma ICU, the nurse talked loudly at her, saying 'Christine, squeeze your mom's hand if you can hear us' and she did.

"She never opened her eyes or responded again. They did an MRI and found she had had a stroke on the left side of her brain. She was in a coma for a week. Then, the doctor sat with us and said the damage was so severe that even if she woke up she would never know anyone was talking to her. "You will have to make a decision," he said.

"I found out from her friends that Christine had been excited thinking we were coming by the restaurant that night. But I didn't call her back when things were crazy at work and we didn't talk all that week. I feel like I let her down. I just feel like I killed my daughter. I feel so much guilt that I didn't talk with her and go to the restaurant like I told her I would. I didn't get to talk to her the last week of her life." Kay wiped the tears from her face.

"She had over 400 people at her funeral. I had no idea how she impacted people's lives. Christine was Christine to me, always sweet and happy. I adored her.

"After she died, I wrote this. It describes what I have felt and learned since her death." Kay gave me a paper with her story on it. What follows is a condensed version of it.

A Hummingbird Named Christine

Yes, this is another story about the sayings "take time to smell the coffee" and "take time to smell the roses." I understood the meaning of those two sayings but I had never felt the meaning in my heart until my 27-year-old daughter, Christine, died in a car accident! My world stopped.

Three months before she died, Christine had placed a beautiful rose-colored ceramic hummingbird feeder just outside the kitchen window. I put the nectar in the feeder the day she brought it home, but never changed it for three months. I'm sure I was just too busy.

A short time after her death, we had a hummingbird visit that beautiful rose-colored feeder. We rarely had them in the summer months and now it was fall. I knew right away it was Christine. Every day, several times a day, the hummingbird would fly in quickly, eat, flutter around for a while and then fly away. That was the life Christine led. She loved to travel and would take off, stay with friends, and then off again. Her life was free flowing with no ties or boundaries, just like this little bird: pretty, delicate and free to fly around where its heart desired, always knowing where home was.

I changed the nectar in the hummingbird feeder every week then, but one day it dawned on me that I couldn't remember the last time I filled the bird and squirrel feeders. I suddenly knew the meaning of take the time to smell and enjoy. We take everything for granted: those birds, the squirrels, the roses and worst of all the people we love so much. They will always be there, we think; how can they not? We try to fill every minute of the day and even use down time to complete another task.

From this tragedy, a beautiful hummingbird named Christine taught me to slow down, take in the smallest of the smalls and value each minute of each day. She valued life to live it her way.

She continued to search for who she was in this big world and home was always home to her. She is still flying free as a hummingbird that comes home to its feeder of fresh nectar. Now I have open eyes that will see the hummingbird and all of its friends in the yard. Open eyes that see the beauty of the smallest of small and hopefully will continue to know what is truly important in life.

If you don't take time to smell the coffee or smell the roses, take time to learn about yourself. You will be amazed at who you meet inside your heart.

Oh what a hummingbird named Christine has taught me. I love you baby girl.

The Repair & Reattachment Grief Therapy

I asked Kay whether she was ready to begin the processing. She agreed and we began.

She decided the most disturbing memory was when the doctor said Christine had severe brain damage. "They said she would never know anyone was talking to her. She wouldn't respond. They told us we had to make a decision. I have so much guilt. I feel like I killed my daughter."

I guided Kay through a set of eye movements and she closed her eyes, focusing on that thought. In a short time, she opened her eyes and said, "I saw Christine lying in bed with a bandage on her head. There was an angel in front of her, and then it went blank. It was totally dark. Then I saw a faint light swirling around my face."

We did more sets of eye movements and Kay described a variety of images. Finally, she opened her eyes after one set and said, "Someone was walking away from me, being led away by another person. The two then stopped and were kneeling, as though praying. Then they flew off, like an angel with her arm around her. I see a lot of angels. I'm seeing angels everywhere. I was just letting her go. I saw someone in a white dress. They were all standing around lifting her up like to heaven. I had the thought, 'Did I finally just let her go?'"

I did another set of eye movements. Kay opened her eyes and said, "My heart is racing. My head is pounding. I heard Christine saying, 'Let me go, Mom. Let me go, Mom.' I felt like I was being pushed back, and then Christine was swimming upstream away from me saying, 'You stay. I'll go.' I asked, 'Why does there have to be a choice?' and she said, 'Because that's the way it is.' I was asking questions, 'Do you want me to take care of your brother?' She said, 'Yes. Take care of Geary.'"

After more eye movements, Kay reported what she experienced: "I said to Christine, 'I miss you' and she said to me, 'I love you, Mom and I'm right here with you.' Then we were being playful and hugging, she and I together, cheek-to-cheek smiling, like we were posing for a picture."

Soon afterward, Kay felt that the connection had faded, so the session ended.

Life Changes from the Repair & Reattachment Grief Therapy

At the beginning of the session, Kay had given a disturbance rating of 10 plus, plus, plus for the memory of the doctor telling her that Christine would never know anyone was talking to her and wouldn't respond. They had to make a decision. Kay felt great guilt. At the end of the session, that had reduced to a 5. The memory of Christine's being in a coma had reduced from a 10 plus, plus, plus to a 2. The memory that she didn't talk to Christine for a week had been a 10 plus, plus. By the end of the session, that had reduced to a 5. Usually the numbers will process even lower on their own over a few days.

Ruth, Joyce's Mom

"You silly goose. Whenever you are thinking of me, I have thought of you before that."

– Ruth, Joyce's mom, in her connection

Joyce came to me for a Repair & Reattachment Grief Therapy with her mom, Ruth. Joyce is an EMDR-certified, licensed social worker who has worked with veterans at the VA for 35 years. She described her life with her mom. "My mom was into the arts. Once a year we went to Chicago and saw a live show like *Gypsy* and *South Pacific*. Mom loved ballroom dancing. She had three partners throughout her lifetime and won ballroom dancing prizes.

"Mom and I did a lot of things together. My brother's wife said I was really dependent on Mom. When I first went to the University of Missouri, Mom went with me to move me into the dorm, and then she stayed in a hotel for a while. I always had to go home for the holidays to be with Mom and Grandma.

"My mom was a chain smoker. My brother and I hounded her to stop smoking, but that just irritated her. She said it was her one and only vice, and she was going to enjoy it. But it took its toll on her. Mom would stop smoking for short periods only when she had edema around her heart. When I was 11 years old, she went into the hospital because of her heart and was there for two months. She seemed to do OK, but never danced after that. Mom's appetite declined and she changed.

"Mom loved dogs. When she was growing up, she had Fluffy. We have a picture of Fluffy doing a trick she taught him. I took an abandoned dog home to Mom and she fell in love with him. She named him Husky. Soon after Husky had settled in, she adopted Roxy. Mom always got Christmas presents for the dogs as well as the family.

"When Mom was in her 60s, she was diagnosed with multiple sclerosis. After that, she didn't work. She had Meals-On-Wheels and regular help, but she went downhill steadily. After a while, she found it difficult to perform even simple tasks. My mom became frustrated with trying to dial a telephone and would have two cigarettes coming out of her mouth. She couldn't figure out how to smoke.

"Still, we'd laugh a lot together. I'd call Mom and we would talk about everything. We were on the same wavelength. We were connected.

"Mom never wanted to go to a nursing home, but my brother made the decision when it was obvious she couldn't live at home. Then, when Mom was 71, I got a call from my sister-in-law at work. She just said, 'Mom's gone.' She died from a bleeder in her brain. I flew to San Jose where my mom lived. My brother and I wanted to see her before she was cremated. I touched her forehead, and my brother and I talked about her being somewhere else, not in her body. My brother and I left her body there. For a long time, I kept wishing Mom was around so I could call her and talk. The last doctor who attended to her when she was still home wrote a letter saying how special she was. He felt like she had made an impact on his life."

The Repair & Reattachment Grief Therapy

After Joyce finished telling me about her mom, we began the Repair & Reattachment Grief Therapy. We targeted various memories for the first part of the session. Many old memories came up. After one set of eye movements, she said, "I could see my brother and me talking. It was so sad. I wanted to have Mom come and live with me, but I was with Terry, my boyfriend, and Mom didn't know him, so she moved to California. I so much wanted to have her live with me. I had dreams of our traveling in an RV around the country."

I said, "Think those words and follow my fingers: 'I wanted Mom to live with me so we would travel in an RV around the country.'" After the eye movements, Joyce opened her eyes and described her connection. "I got a message from Mom. She said, 'You can do the traveling. I will be with you. You tour around the country.' She gave me permission to bring into reality what I wanted for her and me. Mom will be with me. I feel she's close to me even if she's not in this world."

I said, "What would you like to ask her before we close?" Joyce said, "I want to ask her, 'Do you still remember me?'" I guided her through the eye movements and Joyce closed her eyes. When she opened them, she reported, "Mom said to me, 'You silly goose. Whenever you are thinking of me, I have thought of you before that!'"

I said, "Ask her about the picture of Fluffy doing a trick. Would it be OK to use that in the book? We did the eye movements and she reported, "Mom said, 'Yes it certainly would be fine.'"

Joyce's Grandma Emma

"Have some fun and don't work so hard. I want to be part of your having some fun."

– Joyce's Grandma Emma in her connection

Joyce, the VA social worker whose mother came through in the previous chapter, came for a second session to connect with her Grandmother Emma who passed into spirit at 81 years of age. Joyce began the session by telling me about her grandmother.

"Mom, my brother, and I lived with Grandma Emma. Grandma was a nurse, so she was very good at taking care of me as a small child when I was ill. She gave me alcohol baths to cool me down when I had a temperature and would fix our evening meals.

"Mother often went out dancing and Grandma and I would spend nights having black cows made of ice cream and pop. We played a dice game called Bunco and listened to the Grand Ole Opry. When I was five, Grandma walked me to kindergarten the first few days because I was terrified.

"Then, as I grew older, I developed the attitude that Grandma Emma couldn't control me. I called her 'fatso.' Grandma and I

had lots of arguments and physical fights. We shouted nasty, cussing names at each other. Grandma would chase me around the dining room table and push it against the wall to trap me. When I was 10 or 11 years old, it got really bad. One time, I sawed the legs off of her favorite rocking chair. When Grandma saw it, she just cried.

"My mother convinced me to call a truce once a year around Christmas. I always did, and I felt really good during that time. As I got older, Grandma and I mended our relationship and grew close again. She told fortunes at my birthday parties. I remember that and the kids loved it.

"I moved away from home after graduation. In December 1968, I came home to visit and Grandma wasn't there. Mom said she was in the hospital with heart failure. I went to the hospital and found her in an oxygen tent. I held Grandma's hand under the plastic tent and we talked about how much we both hoped she would be home for Christmas. As I held her hand under the plastic tent, I said to her, 'I love you.' I meant it. It was a genuine, heartfelt feeling.

"The next day, we were getting ready to go to the hospital to visit Grandma again when the phone rang. My mother answered the phone, and after listening for a moment, collapsed on the floor sobbing. Grandma Emma had died."

The Repair & Reattachment Grief Therapy

With that, Joyce said she was finished with her story of Grandma Emma, so we began the Repair & Reattachment Grief Therapy. We targeted the memory of Joyce's coming home to find Grandma was not there because she was in the hospital. I asked Joyce, "On a scale of 0 to 10, with 10 being the most disturbing and 0 being none or neutral, how sad, disturbing, or activated was that memory?" She said it was a 9.

I did a set of eye movements and Joyce closed her eyes. When she opened them, she said, "I'm remembering my heart was racing. I was wondering why we weren't going to the hospital right away. My mom wanted to run errands first."

We continued with several more sets of eye movements. Memories of her childhood came up. After one set, she said, "I believe I will see Grandma and my beloved pets again. I live with shadows running around my house. I think it's my dog Joe on the other side. My dogs that live with me now follow the shadows."

I said, "Ask the question, 'Joe, is that you running around the house like a shadow?'" We did the eye movements and she closed her eyes. When she opened them, she said, "I got the message, 'Yes, of course.'"

I said, "Ask Grandma, 'Is there anything you want to say to me before we close?'" I did the eye movements and Joyce described what came to her. "Grandma said 'Have some fun and don't work so hard. I want to be part of your having some fun.'"

Life Changes from the Repair & Reattachment Grief Therapy

At the end of the session, I asked Joyce to tell me, on the scale of 0 to 10, how disturbing it now was to recall the memory of coming home and learning Grandma Emma was in the hospital. She replied, "It's a 2." The memory had greatly diminished in its disturbance for her. The sadness she felt at recalling the memory of her grandma reading palms and telling fortunes at birthday parties was an 8 at the beginning of the session. After the session, it was a 0.

Marie's Grandma

"You get going. Be careful.
I want to see you back in
here real soon."

– Marie's grandma in her connection

Perceived connections can occur during regular psychotherapy sessions with clients who don't even know about the Repair & Reattachment Grief Therapy procedure. I use the eye movements and audio for bilateral stimulation in normal counseling sessions. At times, they open the experiencer to receiving perceived connections. The loved ones involved in the connection are in charge, as well as a wonderful source. When they want to provide loving assistance in a person's life, they may step in for a moment, with remarkably effective consequences for the client.

That is what happened with Marie, a regular client of mine who had no knowledge of, or interest in, having a Repair & Reattachment Grief Therapy. Marie is very industrious. She purchases properties to rent, and repairs and remodels them herself. She also drives an assisted-living van. At the beginning of one psychotherapy session, after she put on the headset with bilateral music and sounds alternating in volume between ears, she said, "I had this dream about my grandmother. She's been gone for years now. I was driving my van and my grandmother appeared in the van. There was cheese all over the floor of the van and I was terribly upset and embarrassed by the mess. My grandma said, 'Let those old folks walk in it. Don't worry about it.'"

Although I wasn't doing a Repair & Reattachment Grief Therapy with Marie, I wanted to see if some insights from her grandma might help her in our psychotherapy session. So I said, "OK, let's try this, Marie. Ask your grandma, 'Was that you in my dream?'" I did a set of eye movements and Marie closed her eyes. When she opened them, she said, "I just asked, 'Was that you in my dream, Grandma?' And she answered! I could hear Grandma's voice saying, 'Of course it was me. I miss you. I haven't seen you for so long. You need to come and see me more often. I miss your stories. There was always something new happening in your life.'"

I did another set of eye movements and when Marie opened her eyes, she reported, "Grandma said, 'You need to make more time for me. You and Robin [her sister] are my favorite girls. You are my sweetie.'"

It was time to end the session. Unlike the Repair & Reattachment Grief Therapy that go on until the loved ones involved in the connection end them, my regular client time is an hour session. I said to Marie, "Ask your grandma if there is anything she wants to say before we close today." After a set of eye movements, she closed her eyes. When she opened them, she said, "I asked Grandma, and she said 'Yes. You get going. Be careful. I want to see you back in here real soon.'"

When Marie came in for her next regular psychotherapy session, we targeted some things that were upsetting her, as we normally do. I used the audio bilateral stimulation and eye movements. Each time I guided her through the eye movements, she focused on the things that were upsetting her.

She was saying toward the end of the session, "I have to learn to step back. I just need to step back. I want to change and I want to get there." I had her focus on that while I guided her through a set of the eye movements. When she opened her eyes, she said excitedly, "Grandma came in again! Grandma said, 'Don't worry about it now. It will come down the road. You'll know what to do. Just don't worry about it. I'll help you when I can.' Oh, my gosh, Grandma is talking to me! She's talking to me!"

Grandma is determined to come through in love to help her granddaughter. I expect her to make more appearances during Marie's normal psychotherapy sessions.

Marie Overcomes a Tragedy in Another Session

When Marie walked in for her next regular session, she was obviously upset. She said something happened that she needed help with. I had her sit and put on the headphones to prepare for a psychotherapy session. When she was ready, she told me, "One of my tenants was found dead."

Marie owned and maintained rental properties for her parents. She continued, "One of the tenants called me saying they had found another tenant, Daniel, dead in his apartment. The police had come and taken his body away. I went up to the apartment, but I didn't want to go in. I felt like Daniel was outside of the apartment when I went up to the door. Sally, the tenant who called me, was standing outside the door. She said, 'I'll go in with you.' We went in and the bed was perfectly made. As I passed the bedroom corner, I could feel his energy was there. In another room, there was a very angry letter venting about how despondent he felt."

I said, "Just notice that and follow my fingers." I did a set of eye movements and Marie closed her eyes. She said, "I can feel a presence behind me. There's an angel holding Daniel. There's peace." We targeted that with another set of eye movements. She said, "He was tired. He's telling me he was lonesome, estranged, angry, and frustrated."

I did another set of eye movements while Marie focused on that. When she opened her eyes, she said, "I asked him, 'Daniel, was that you I felt outside of the apartment when I walked up to it?' I heard, 'Absolutely.' He said he felt sorry about the letter. He was depressed and unhappy and lashing out."

We did another set of eye movements. When Marie opened her eyes, she said, "I felt what he was doing. He was so frustrated he needed help. That corner in his bedroom embraced him and it was comfortable. And that is where he died."

After another set of eye movements, she said, "I couldn't tell where I was. I was floating. It felt peaceful and light. I was floating past Bend, Oregon, and I could see Daniel. I floated down to Austin, Texas, where his daughter Becky lives, like he was taking me there. And then I heard Daniel saying, 'Tell Becky and my ex-wife Laura how I felt. Tell them here there's compassion, love, forgiveness, and being able to let go.'"

I did another set of eye movements. Marie said, "I felt calm and was floating again. It felt soft and comfortable. I could hear Daniel. He said, 'Take your time, go slow. Don't get overwhelmed with all of your finances and this experience you've been through with me. It will all fall into place. Take one step at a time.' Then he told me, 'I didn't mean to die in your apartment. I didn't know where to go. I just wanted to disappear in a corner.'"

Then Marie said, "I felt like my thoughts were floating again, back into the apartment. The corner where Daniel passed away has turned into a comfortable cradle to me. It feels soft and downy in that corner. It is so different for me now. I'm getting from him now that he's in a better place."

I said, "Marie, ask him if there's anything he wants to say before we close." I did the eye movements and she reported, "Yes. He said, 'Number one, my daughter Becky needs to be comforted. Two, there's not enough love and not enough compassion in the world. I'm sorry you were involved in this, Marie but there's not enough love, there is not enough compassion in this world."

With that, the session ended.

Life Changes from the Repair & Reattachment Grief Therapy

At the beginning of the session, when Marie rated the memory of learning that Daniel had died in her apartment building, she rated it a 10 plus for being disturbing to her. I asked her to rate the memory after the session; it had reduced to 0.

When she left my office, Marie was a different person. She wasn't upset and sad like she was when she came into my office. She felt comforted and even felt good that Daniel came to her to explain what happened and give her good advice.

Marie came in a week later for her regular session. She said, "There's a really interesting thing I wanted to tell you about. After Daniel died, I was very worried because I already had an apartment vacant, so then I had two apartments for which I wouldn't receive rent this month. On top of that, I had an empty space in my office building. I wasn't going to be able to pay the mortgage without the money from those three rentals. Then I thought about what Daniel said: 'Don't get overwhelmed with all of your finances. It will all fall into place.' Immediately, that helped me relax and not be so worried.

"A short time after that, I got a call and rented the other apartment. The next day, I had a renter for Daniel's apartment, and yesterday, I got a renter for the office space! Daniel was right. I didn't need to feel overwhelmed. It all fell into place."

Pete, April's Dad

"All the generations are there. Daddy's with the family he loves so much, and he's content."

— April, during her connection with her dad, Pete

April came to me to help her connect with her father, Pete, who died in 2007 at age 86. "Daddy was a really soft-spoken, gentle, kind person," she said, "but he and I didn't really have a relationship. When I was growing up, Daddy was focused on Mom. When I was a little girl, Mom would say, 'Daddy loves me best, and I love you best.' I grew up thinking he didn't care much about me.

"I was an only child until I was 15, when they adopted Dawn. Daddy had some reservations about it, but they did it anyway.

They arranged to adopt her before she was born and traveled to Nebraska to get her. I adored Dawn.

"I got married at 16 years of age. My dad didn't say anything that I can remember about my getting married that young. My husband was going to college in a different city, so we lived there. Once, when I was leaving my parents' house to take the train back home, I leaned over to kiss Dawn goodbye and Daddy kissed me on the cheek. He never did that before. I was still thinking about that when I got on the train, and I started crying. I felt so alone.

"When he was in his 80s, Daddy had a series of health problems. He had knee replacement surgery, two blood clots that went to his lungs, a heart condition, and pneumonia. Daddy started to get better, but then suffered a cardiac arrest.

"The doctors decided that they would put a defibrillator in him. At this time, Mom was getting Alzheimer's and dementia. She signed herself into another hospital, so I was orchestrating people to be sure there would be someone with one of them every day. Several times during Mom and Dad's illnesses, Daddy said, 'April, I don't know what we would do without you.' That was very touching to me.

"When Mom and Daddy were about to be discharged from the hospitals, we realized that neither would be able to manage living in their home, so my daughter found a care-home facility for them. It was very sad. They never saw their home again. That was hard on my dad because he was very independent.

"Eventually, Daddy was in such pain that he returned to the hospital for tests. The doctor told me they had found mesothelioma, a form of lung cancer caused by inhaling asbestos. He said that Daddy had just a few weeks or a month to live. When Daddy was discharged from the hospital, he and Mom stayed with me for a week. Then we took Daddy to hospice. They put him on morphine because of the severe pain. It was hard to leave him in the hospice room that night.

"We went back to Daddy's room the next day. The nurse said that he had been sleeping all morning. On the following day, the nurse called at 7 a.m. She said, 'It's time for someone to be here.' When we arrived, the nurse was giving Daddy breathing treatments. He said, 'I'm having hallucinations. I see dots and I see people.' I asked him, 'Who do you see?' and he started crying.

"My sister and I stayed with Daddy. He slept a lot. My two daughters came when we let them know the severity of Daddy's condition. Daddy said, 'I think I'm going to have to go.' I said, 'It's OK, Daddy. You'll be there when it's our turn.' He said softly, 'I know, but I don't want to go.' We said, 'We'll take care of Mom.' My mom, even through her Alzheimer's, said, 'I'll be OK.' Daddy grabbed Mom's arm and held onto it. My sister and I said, 'It's OK to go, Daddy.' The nurse put morphine on his tongue and he fell asleep. He never woke up again.

"His respirations were eleven a minute. I was sitting in his chair watching his blanket rise and fall when he breathed. After a while, the blanket stopped moving and I thought, 'I think he's gone.'

"My sister called the mortuary in the town where they lived and he was transported there. The graveside service was a military funeral, just as he wanted. His cousin's son played 'Taps' and military representatives were there. They stood before Mom and saluted her. That was very touching.

"I picked the songs that played during the service: 'Remember You are Loved,' 'No One Ever Prepares Us for This,' 'Goodbye, My Mother, Father,' 'You Are Wonderful,' 'You Are an Angel,' and 'I'm Going to Raise You Up.'

"I read the poem, 'When Great Trees Fall' at his service.

The Repair & Reattachment Grief Therapy

April had finished telling me about her dad. After a short break, we began the Repair & Reattachment Grief Therapy procedure. We started with the memory, "They never went back home," which she had rated as a 10 plus, plus, plus for disturbance. I guided April through a set of eye movements and she closed her eyes. When she opened them, she said, "I saw the trailer exactly as Mom had left it, with the covers pulled back. Daddy's little room with his TV was neat and clean, just as though they were going to come back home someday. Then I heard the soothing sound of waves coming from the headset. I was thinking, 'This is how Daddy is feeling now. He's in a serene place watching the waves.'"

I did another set of eye movements and April described what she experienced: "I saw the silhouette of a farm in Nebraska, like the end of a movie with all the people in his family who have passed. They're home. Daddy is home. Then I saw him running through the cornfields. Running through the cornfields was all he could do that was peaceful and fun as he was growing up. When he was a teenager, he had to take care of his dad, who had a mental breakdown. Then he married my mom, who had mental and emotional problems. Daddy's life was hard. Running through the cornfields was the last memory my dad had of peace and fun. He is able to run through the cornfields again now."

I saw April breathing heavily and jerking. She was releasing pent-up energy from her body that she had been carrying for years. Relaxing allowed the connection to unfold. She said, "I remember on one of Daddy's last days, I came into the hospice room and Daddy got this big grin on his face, like 'There's my daughter.' My sister noticed it too."

I did another set of eye movements with April and she said, "I saw Daddy a lot younger, maybe 32 years old, with khaki work clothes on. There was a fog behind him and he was smiling at me. Then I saw his brothers and sisters gathered around him. Daddy isn't alone and doesn't have to do anything alone again. All the generations are there. Daddy's with the family he loves so much, and he's content."

After another set of eye movements, she reported, "Daddy said, 'I know you have felt alone all your life. All these people are here for you and love you.' He said he feels total acceptance and belonging there. Then he said to me, 'The things you have felt your whole life alone, April, you will feel differently. You will feel a sense of acceptance and belonging. When you feel like you are alone and don't belong, think of this vision of me and of everyone here, going back and back and back for generations. You are a part of us.'"

I guided her through another set of eye movements and she continued. "I first saw myself at seven or eight years old, climbing trees and riding bicycles by myself. I felt sad for the little girl who was alone. I saw myself running through the cornfields without a care in the world, like my dad did."

I asked April how disturbing the memory was now of her mom and dad leaving their home, never to go back. It had been a 10 plus, plus, plus at the beginning of the session. She said, "Now it's a zero."

We started targeting a new memory. It was, "I grew up thinking that Daddy didn't care that much about me." I did the eye movements with April and she closed her eyes. When she opened them, she said, "I'm getting answers. First, back when I was leaving my parents' house to take the train home and Daddy kissed me on the cheek, I never realized how hard that was for him, and I didn't appreciate it at a time. I understand and appreciate that more now.

"The second thing was that maybe the reason he had reservations about adopting was that he was concerned about how it would affect me." I said, "Ask the question, 'Was the reason you had reservations about adopting a baby that you were concerned about how it might affect me?' We did the eye movements and her dad came through right away. April told me, "He said, 'It should have been the reason,' but I got that it had more to do with Daddy's life with Mom. He said he knows everything now. He can see! He told me that understanding what he knows now, the adoption's effect on me should have been the reason that he had reservations about adopting."

I asked April, "How disturbing now is the memory that you grew up thinking your dad didn't care much about you." She replied immediately: "Zero!"

I said to April, ask your dad, "Is there anything else you would like to tell me that you think will make me feel better?" I did a set of the eye movements and when she opened her eyes she said, "I was hearing music that sounded kind of sad to me. That's what Daddy's passing was like. Then the sadness diminished, and the music felt like it represented where he is now. I heard the music as being like the good feeling you might get when a storm ends and the worst part of the storm is over. Daddy's at the crescendo. He's at the most magnificent part of the music!"

With that, April's Repair & Reattachment Grief Therapy with her dad ended.

Life Changes from the Repair & Reattachment Grief Therapy

April began the session feeling that the memory of realizing her mom and dad would never go back home was very disturbing for her. She rated it a 10 plus, plus, plus. During the session, that reduced to a 0. She had rated the memory that she grew up thinking her dad didn't care much about her as a 10 plus, plus, plus. It also had reduced to a 0.

Madeline, Melissa's Friend

"It really doesn't matter where
your ashes are when you're gone, but
thank you for thinking of me."

– Madeline to Melissa in her connection

Melissa came to my office to have a Repair & Reattachment Grief Therapy focusing on her friend, Madeline, who died at 50 from cancer. "I met Madeline at a professional meeting," Melissa said. "We hit it off immediately and eventually became close friends. We were both single, loved dogs, and did things with the dogs together. Madeline was easygoing, friendly, and very spiritual.

"Several years after I met her, Madeline was diagnosed with cancer. She had no family close by, so I went through the ordeal with her. She had surgeries to remove the cancer, but they couldn't get all of it.

"She tried various treatments to rid her body of the cancer, or at least slow its growth. Each failed. The cancer kept growing. After several months, Madeline was becoming weaker, and we knew she would soon be leaving us. We did everything we could to take care of her, but the cancer progressed in spite of our efforts. As she neared the end, a relative of hers moved into the house to care for her. Finally, her body could fight no more, and we knew the end was near. Her friends and relatives came to her room to be with her. As her breathing became more labored and her eyes closed to a tiny slit, we all gathered around her bed. Madeline breathed her last, gentle breath, and was gone.

"Her brother stood with us in the circle around her, holding his one-year old son. The little boy kept looking at the ceiling saying, 'Light, light.' We all looked at each other, knowing it was Madeline leaving.

"After a while, I stepped away from the bed and walked out into Madeline's garden where the roses she cared for and loved were in bloom. I picked some, took them inside, and put them around her on the bed. I remembered she had a toy halo with streamers coming down, so I found it and put it on her head.

"After her cremation, we talked about where to spread her ashes and finally decided to spread them around in the places she had loved. We did so, but I had a little bit left over, so I put it in my dresser drawer to keep part of her close to me. One day I walked by the dresser and heard a voice say, 'Let me out of here!' So I took the little portion of ashes and spread them outside."

The Repair & Reattachment Grief Therapy

Melissa had ended her story about her friend Madeline, so I began the Repair & Reattachment Grief Therapy procedure. After the first set of eye movements, Melissa closed her eyes. The connection began immediately. When she opened her eyes, she said, "I heard Madeline. She was saying, 'I knew I wasn't going to make it, but you made it better. Your gift to me was taking care of me.' And I suddenly realized it was really a gift to us. I was learning how to care for someone."

I guided her through a set of eye movements. Melissa reported, "I got the message that there are some changes happening in my profession and she wants to help me make them. She said the book I'm writing about it is a segue. 'Let it evolve,' she said. 'You don't need to do anything. Let it come up. I will be there to help you.'"

After another set of eye movements, Melissa described what she experienced while her eyes were closed, "I saw Madeline with her shaggy dog Brutus, who was killed. And Pal and Pokie were there. They died years ago. I'm seeing them all right now, and Madeline looks really happy. She said to me, 'When you come over here, you get to hang out with your old dogs. I'll be here and we can hang out together.' We used to always do things together with our dogs."

We did another set of eye movements. When Melissa opened her eyes, she said "I saw Madeline's stepmother, who's deceased, in a big hat with a wide brim, smiling. Then Madeline told me about a friend of mine who died a month ago. She said, 'She's much happier here than she was there. She's laughing now too.'"

After another set of eye movements, Melissa said, "Madeline told me when I see a rainbow to think of her. It's her way of saying, 'Hello.' Madeline said to me, 'It really doesn't matter where your ashes are when you're gone, but thank you for thinking of me. Goodbye. I'll see you over here.'"

We did a set of eye movements to see whether Madeline had anything more to say. She did. Melissa reported that she said, 'What a powerful spirit your mother is. She's around you to keep you in line and make sure you notice her. She's always around you.' Then I saw Grandma, Mom, Madeline, and Arny, my husband, all there ready to answer questions. They all seemed to be giving me the message, 'Why do you always ask if you're making this up? It's not what you anticipated, is it?'"

I said to Melissa, "Ask them if they have anything to say about the Repair & Reattachment Grief Therapy and where you fit in." I did the eye movements and she closed her eyes. When she opened them, she said, "What I got was 'A good process. This helps us communicate without being filtered through someone else like a medium.' They said my part is learning to do it quickly and working with people to keep the process going. 'It will all unfold in its own time,' they said. 'It's really good that you and Rochelle connected.'"

I did another set of eye movements, and when Melissa opened her eyes, she said they spoke about the conference Melissa and I were going to in a few months, where we would speak about Repair & Reattachment Grief Therapy. "You will end up going to the conference," they said to her. "The money will be there. Keep the communication going every day like you have been doing, through writing. You have important things to do in your work with people. Your work and the Repair & Reattachment Grief Therapy will come together in a way you and Rochelle haven't thought of. Communicate with the spirit you married, not the one that you're divorcing." They were referring to communicating with Arny on their side of life, not the man she was in the process of divorcing when we did the Repair & Reattachment Grief Therapy. "The writing process you do," they said to her, "can be used for this spirit you married who is on this side of life." Then Melissa said they spoke about this *Repair & Reattachment Grief Therapy* book. They said, "The book will be a huge success, but not right away when it first comes out. It will evolve into something really big."

Melissa wanted to ask a question, "Will I be happier where my office is now, and will I get enough work?" So we did another set of eye movements. After Melissa opened her eyes, she said they told her, "You will have more work than you can do. It will be connecting with people and helping them rather than doing research. It's a whole different world. It's a system to help people."

We did a final set of eye movements focusing on the question, "Is there anything else you want to say?" When she opened her eyes, she said the answer was, "Continue the communication."

Life Changes from the Repair & Reattachment Grief Therapy

I asked Melissa to bring up the memories we started with to see how much effect they had on her now. The one that she rated most highly disturbing was a 0 now. The other that she rated as a 7 had reduced to a 2.

KG, Virginia's Husband

"It is important that you love yourself. Take care of yourself so life can be as full as possible."

– KG to Virginia during her connection

Virginia came to me to have a connection with her husband KG, who passed away at the age of 54.

"I met KG one night at a nightclub where I often went to dance," Virginia began. "We spent the whole evening talking and soon became friends. He wanted to marry me. I really didn't want to marry KG because I had just been married to a biker named Chuck who was stabbed to death at a biker bar, leaving me with a 9-month-old child. I didn't want to go through another marriage. But KG kept asking me and after five tries, finally wore me down. We had 30+ wonderful years of marriage. We were best friends.

"KG was very intelligent and could do many things. He became an Army nurse after we were married and a carpenter when he was discharged. He moved up to being a contractor and worked in construction for 20 years. He could build anything. I'd design things and he would build them. We built everything together.

"We just had a lot of fun. We joined a club in which we studied how people in different periods of history lived and the music they listened to. One of our favorites was medieval times. We would camp with other members, living in tents as the people did in those periods. We loved the many great friends we met and new adventures we experienced. Our favorite part was cooking feasts in the great halls for gatherings of hundreds of people.

"In later years KG and I spent time having cookouts and playing games with a smaller circle of friends, camping on the property of a friend who lived next to us. KG and I had beautiful memories of our time there.

"But when KG was in his 50s, his hepatitis C got worse, and his health deteriorated until he had great difficulty participating in the activities we loved so much. Life changed. Earlier in our lives, we adopted two beautiful Rottweiler dogs, Ruby and Gypsy, who were like children to me. As time passed, they too grew old and my family had to put them down one at a time. That was so very hard. I was in so much grief.

"I am so very grateful that every single day KG and I would kiss and we would say, 'I love you' to each other. One morning when KG was 54 years old, we said 'I love you,' as usual, and I drove off to work, but it wasn't long before my son called to tell me KG had had an aneurism and was in the hospital. I drove to the hospital and found him in the ICU on life support. He never regained consciousness and soon died. When he died, I lost all my faith. Half of me was gone.

"Then, about a year ago, my kidneys failed and I had to go on dialysis. I was very, very sick, and very, very scared. I didn't have KG to comfort me. They put in a chest catheter to dialyze me. I knew I could die at any time from renal failure. It has been very hard for me to adjust. I constantly have to choose the right foods and do the right things, and I'm worried I'm going to do something wrong. It's overwhelming and scary. I got to where I didn't care if I lived or died.

"Now, it makes me sad to go back to our property because KG and our Rottweilers are no longer there. I have to go back to clean out 30+ years of memories, but it's hard. The things we always shared, they're not possible now. Sometimes it's hard for me to feel happy and get involved in anything. Before, with KG, life had color and brightness. Now it's bleak and dark. I miss him so much sometimes I can't get beyond that. I'm afraid the sadness keeps me from enjoying life. I have moments that I just know I am really depressed."

The Repair & Reattachment Grief Therapy

When Virginia was ready, we started the Repair & Reattachment Grief Therapy procedure. We targeted the memory she rated a 10, the highest rating for being disturbing. The thought was, "I can't recapture it. I feel depressed." I said, "Think those words, bring up the image or the picture that goes with them, and watch my fingers." I did the eye movements and told her to go inside with that memory. When she opened her eyes, she said, "I feel helpless, alone and vulnerable. I feel numb and devoid of feelings."

I could see Virginia releasing energy. Her right foot was moving back and forth. I did another set of eye movements. She said, "I no longer feel alone. I feel hopeful. The feelings have shifted." She said she also saw a yellow fluid movement cross in front of her eyes. She told me later that this was KG's favorite color. "He painted our whole bedroom yellow," she said. She was beginning to go beyond the sadness.

We did a set of eye movements and the connection began. When she opened her eyes she said, "I was telling KG that he is still alive in our hearts and minds and we have not forgotten him, but it's also important for us to know that he has not forgotten us. He said to me, 'It's important for you to know that you are also alive in my heart and mind and memories.' Rochelle, I'm overflowing with love. I feel like I want to dance. I can't stop smiling."

I guided her through more eye movements and she closed her eyes. Tears began to flow gently down her cheeks. "I am crying but it's more for joy than sadness," she said. After another set of eye movements, she closed her eyes and began to breathe deeply, moving around in her chair. She was releasing more old pent-up energy she had been carrying that had kept her depressed. She said, "It was such a joy to know him. I was so lucky."

She described an unusual dreamlike experience she had about KG soon after he died. I said, "Ask the question, 'Was that you I saw in the dream?'" I did a set of eye movements and she said, "'Yes,' he said, 'It was.'"

Their daughter was married a few months after the funeral, and their son dreamed that KG was present at the wedding. She asked him if he was really there and he said, "Of course I was."

We examined another highly disturbing area of her life: her kidney failure. After another set of eye movements, she said, "I am not afraid of it anymore. I'm proud of the way I have handled it. I'm happy and hopeful; my body is strong."

Virginia swayed in her chair, with tears flowing down her cheeks. She pointed at her face and said, "These are happy tears." I said, "Ask a final question: 'KG, is there anything you want to say before we stop today?'" I did a set of eye movements, and when she opened her eyes she said, "Yes, he did have something to say. He said, 'I'm so very proud of you. It's important that you love yourself and take care of yourself so life can be as full as possible.' I feel blissful. I just feel blissful."

Life Changes from the Repair & Reattachment Grief Therapy

During the session, I said to Virginia, "Bring up the thought, 'I can't recapture it. I feel depressed.' How would you rate that thought now on the scale of 0 to 10?" She said, "I can't bring it to mind. Now, it's a zero because I'm filled with joy!"

I said, "You rated the disturbance you felt with the thought about the kidney failure as a 9.5 at the beginning. Where is it now?" She said, "It's a 2. I'm hopeful, happy and not afraid to die. Before, I was afraid. Now my life is full of reasons to wake up in the morning. I just have to remember that."

She had rated her fear of the dialysis and renal failure and her scare that she might not be making the right choices about food and activities as a 9 at the beginning. After the processing, I said, "What is that now?" She said, "It's a 4.5."

She had rated the thought, "Life has no brightness without KG," as a 9 for disturbance at the beginning. During the session, she said it had reduced to a 3. She said, "I am grateful for what I had. How fortunate I was to have found the love of my life. Some people never get that chance. That makes me want to remember only the beautiful moments. The joy I have had outweighs the sadness."

The thought, "I miss him so much I can't get beyond that," had been a 9. During the session, she said, "It's zero because I can get beyond it now. I do believe I will be able to find the color in my life again. I want to remember the joy and the goodness. I feel such joy in this moment."

When the session ended, she said to me, "I'm in a state of bliss. Thank you."

Sandy, Shawn's Mom

"I'm OK!"

– Sandy to her son, Shawn, during their connection

Shawn was referred to me for panic attacks and post-traumatic stress disorder (PTSD) from combat in Somalia and the Gulf War. He was unable to sleep through the night and was feeling very stressful in his job, but didn't know what to do about it. I did some work with him on the panic attacks and PTSD, and in the process, I learned that his mother had died 26 years earlier in a car accident. He was 12 years old at the time, and although he didn't seem to be grieving for her, I believed that his panic attacks might be exacerbated by some underlying grief.

I said, "I believe your panic attacks may be affected by your mother's death. I know a new way to work with grief and loss. We can either continue working on your panic attacks using EMDR, or we can try it this new way for two sessions. He agreed, saying, "Let's try it the new way," so we did. EMDR (eye movement desensitization and reprocessing) is the standard therapy method that uses eye movements. The new way I was referring to is a Repair & Reattachment Grief Therapy.

I asked him to tell me about his mother, especially the accident and her death. And so he began. "My mom's name was Sandy. She was a stay-at-home mom and I was her favorite, even though I was adopted. I had a really good relationship with Mom. I never saw her get mad. She was really easygoing. She loved Elvis Presley and Buddy Holly.

"She was 33 years old when she died. Mom and I were driving to town to get our truck fixed because the power steering pump had gone out. The roads were windblown and icy. We were on a road that had waves in it because the roadway had settled. As we drove, my mom got a cramp in her foot and bent down to massage it out. At that moment, we hit one of the waves in the road and started sliding. Mom over-corrected the steering and the truck flipped end over end seven times. She was thrown out and the truck hit her. A truck driver who saw the accident pulled me out of the window and got a blanket for my mom. She was lying on the ground moaning. An ambulance came and I rode to the hospital with her. At the hospital, they took her into a room to work on her. In a little while, the doctor came out and said, 'I'm sorry.' That's all I remember about the hospital.

"At the funeral there were tons of people and lots of food. I remember special cake that I ate. I was pretty sore but I was walking around. I remember just staying away from everyone. They flew up an Elvis tribute singer for the funeral from Las Vegas. He sang a lot of Mom's favorite Elvis songs. Then they put Mom in a mausoleum. I go every other year to put flowers there."

The Repair & Reattachment Grief Therapy

When Shawn finished telling me about his mom, I began the Repair & Reattachment Grief Therapy procedure. We decided that the most disturbing memory was when the doctor at the hospital said, "I'm sorry," and Shawn knew that his mom had died. He rated that as a 10 on the scale of the disturbance scale of 0 to 10. It made him very sad to think of it.

I did a series of the eye movements with him, and after each one, he closed his eyes for a while, then opened them to describe what he experienced. At first, the experiences were focused on the hospital and accident. Then, after a number of these procedures, the connection happened, dramatically. He opened his eyes and said he heard his mother's voice distinctly saying, really loudly, "I'm OK." "I felt heat all over my back," he said. I later told him that that was her presence. The connection was very short, but the effect was profound.

Life Changes from the Repair & Reattachment Grief Therapy

At the end of the session, I asked Shawn how disturbing the memory of the doctor at the hospital saying "I'm sorry" when his mom died was for him. It was a 10 at the beginning of the session. He said it had reduced to a 1.

Two months later, I spoke with Shawn on the phone. He said, "The night after the connection was the first night I can remember sleeping the entire night through. Now, every night, I stay asleep all night. I'm feeling much better. I can't believe I feel so much better from doing this. I didn't think my mom's death affected me that much now.

"And I quit working at the post office and started a new career. I'm really happy now."

His simple message from Mom changed his life.

Rose, Lauren's Mom

"Someday, Lauren, we will understand it all."

– A message to Lauren during her connection with her mother

Lauren is a social worker with the Veterans Administration.
Her mother, Rose, passed into spirit at 85 years of age. Lauren
came to my office to have a Repair & Reattachment Grief Therapy
with her mother one morning at 10:30 a.m. We continued the
Repair & Reattachment Grief Therapy until 4 p.m. This is a
summary of the story she told me about her mom, Rose.

"Mom was a little girl during the Great Depression. Her dad
left the family when she was young and Grandma raised her and
her siblings in great poverty. One day in school, Mom's teacher
told her she had to clean up before coming to school, because her
arms were caked with dirt.

"Mom had respiratory problems her whole life. As a child,
she had tuberculosis and she smoked until she was 55 or 60 years
old. She used a breathing machine her last year of life. She told
us it was for her asthma, but we knew it was emphysema.

"Mom was obsessive-compulsive. Every room in the house
had a bottle of disinfectant and rollers to pick up lint. She had to
control everything, including me, but that didn't mean she was
able to manage issues well. I had a burning stomach all the way
through high school and in college, but she didn't do anything to
treat it.

"My father, Ben, was killed when I
was 15-months old in World War II. We
lived with my grandmother, Mom's
mother, until Mom got a job. Mom began
to date Paul, and they married when I
was nine years old. They had a baby girl,
Tina, and two years later, another baby
girl, Sally.

"I became the built-in babysitter. I
loved babies, and did a lot of work, taking
care of them like a full-time nanny. But
Mom never made me get up at night
when they needed something.

"My younger sister, Sally, had chickenpox and high fever.
When we took her to the doctor, they diagnosed her as having

developmentally delayed disorder. Mom blamed herself for
Sally's retardation and said she didn't want another baby. She
was overwhelmed with two babies and was always complaining
about what a nuisance everything was. I was in junior high
school, so she had to drive me around to events and complained
about what a burden that was.

"Paul had promised to give me a
pony because I loved to ride other
people's ponies. But they had
limited income when they married
because Paul was still sending
money to his mother, so I never did
get my own pony.

"At the same time, Mom was
having problems with Paul's parents, her in-laws. They
continually gave her grief, and Mom responded by pointing out
every fault they had. I don't think she told Paul how she felt, but
there was nothing good between them.

"I left for college, and when I came home, things had become
really bad. Mom was taking Valium and drinking a lot to cope.
Paul would blow up at her and they'd argue. They went to a
priest for marriage counseling, but Mom got no help from that.
The priest said she needed to be a better wife.

"Mom was very needy and began clinging to me. After I
graduated from college, I came home one Christmas and as I was
leaving, Mom said, 'Why do we even have kids when they just
leave?' Sally's teacher talked to me about Sally's condition and
said, 'Do you have to go? Sally needs you.'

"My mom's mother, my grandmother, lived with her new
husband, Lester. Lester was always good to me. But Grandma
died, and only a year later, Lester died of a broken heart. After
Grandma's and Lester's deaths, Mom wouldn't talk to me for
several years. I couldn't understand it; I was just numb. I called
mom 7 or 8 years later when I had my first baby, and she was
pretty friendly. We started talking more.

"At the time, I was going through a divorce and was seeing a psychiatrist to get me through the rough spots. He was a great help to me. But then he died. I was upset and told Mom, crying, that he had passed away. She said, 'You don't need to cry. So what? Why are you crying over a psychiatrist? You don't need him and you don't need to cry either.' She didn't like men. She wasn't very nice to my son and made snide comments about his picture with his ponytail.

"But Mom did have a warm spot in her heart. I went to her house a few weeks before she died to take her to the store. As I was helping her get dressed, I was down on the floor putting her shoes on and she said, 'Your father and I did one good thing' and she looked straight at me, smiling.

"Then, one afternoon when I came home from work, my sister Tina called. 'Mom's in the hospital,' she said. 'I'm here with her now.' Tina continued, 'Mom asked me, "Am I really going to die?" I said, 'Yes, we all are, and you're going to see your mom.'" That evening, Tina called to tell me that Mom had passed away. We had a Mass at church in Los Angeles. Through my tears I read something that I had come to learn about my mom. It was titled 'My Mom Had Guts.' This was a woman of courage."

The Repair & Reattachment Grief Therapy

We began the Repair & Reattachment Grief Therapy procedure with the memory that was a 10 plus, plus, plus, that her mom hated men and treated her son badly. I did a set of the eye movements and Lauren closed her eyes. When she opened them, she described seeing her mom's father coming through a door at her grandma's house, complaining about aches and pains and constipation. Then she said, "Everyone is so critical. Mom and Grandma were so critical of him."

I said, focus on that and follow my fingers. I did the eye movements. When Lauren opened her eyes, she said, "I saw a picture my aunt had given me with four generations of the women in our family and my uncle as a little boy. The women all looked stern and mean."

I did several more sets of eye movements. With each set, she described scenes from her childhood with her grandma. All the while, she was sighing, yawning, and breathing deeply. She was releasing pent-up energy connected to the memories.

Then, after a set of eye movements, Lauren opened her eyes and said, "It's flipped to Grandma. Grandma and I are cooking breakfast. We're making pancakes." She shifted her weight and said, "I feel restless in my chair." She let out a big yawn, releasing more energy.

I did another set of eye movements and the connection began. When Lauren opened her eyes, she said, "I saw her. I said, 'Is that you, Grandma?' I heard her say, 'Damn it, Lauren. You know it. You see me.' I said to her, 'You were dead but you are alive.'" Lauren was shifting in her chair, releasing more energy.

We did more eye movements. Lauren said, "I saw the front door to Grandma's house, and it was open. I asked Grandma, 'Why is the front door open? It was always closed in the good old days. Why is it open?' Grandma answered that she didn't know, and I said, 'Well, who can we ask? Why was it open? Was it the wind?' Grandma said to me, 'You don't need to ask anybody. It's an open door. People come. People go. You just need to answer your own questions.'"

We did another set of eye movements. Lauren reported, "I saw Grandma again. I saw her dead and alive. She was on the back porch, then out in the front. The door was open, and it was so light. Things just feel open."

I said to Lauren, "Ask Grandma, 'Is there anything you want to tell me about all of this?'" We did a set of eye movements and she said, "Grandma told me, 'We're all with you, Lauren.'" A look of realization formed on her face. "Of course, that's the meaning of the doors. I had a dream last week and in it there was an open door. I sensed that it was an open door between two worlds. Now she's saying to me, 'It doesn't matter how it opened.' Rochelle, it doesn't seem possible. How do I know that about the doors that were in my dream and the open doors I just saw in Grandma's house?"

I said, "Don't question it. Stay with that thought," and I did another set of eye movements. When Lauren opened her eyes, she said, "I asked Grandma, 'Where the hell is my mom? Why isn't she showing up in this connection?' The answer I got was, 'We are all with you.'"

I said to Lauren, "Do you have anything you want to ask your Grandma?" She replied, "Yes, I want to ask for a sign that Mom and Dad are around." I did another set of eye movements and Lauren closed her eyes. When she opened them, she reported, "Grandma said to me, 'Lauren, I told you we're all with you. Have I ever lied to you, Lauren? The door is open. We can go in and we can go out.'" Lauren said to me, "Rochelle, in the dream, Grandma was breathing. It meant you can be alive and dead. There is a piece of me that doubted, but I never expected to hear those words."

I guided her through another set of eye movements and Lauren said, with her eyes closed, "I think I'm hearing my mother." She was sighing repeatedly and moving in her chair for some time, releasing energy. When she opened her eyes, she said "I heard her voice say 'I criticized Lauren because I thought I was horrible.' I don't know where the voice was coming from.'"

I said to Lauren, "Don't judge it or try to figure it out." She continued, "Then I heard Mom's voice say, 'I do have a gang around here.'"

I said, "Stay with that thought and follow my fingers." We did a set of eye movements. When she opened her eyes, she said, "I heard Mom's voice. 'I have the gang,' she said again. Then I saw my psychiatrist and I saw Dad and I saw Grandma and more people. It really was a gang! Wow. Then the image of the harp came up. I'll be starting harp lessons next week. That's a really positive image."

I said, "Do you want to ask them any questions?" She answered, "Yes. I want to ask my dad, 'Where do they see me going my second and third trimesters of my life?'"

I guided her through a set of eye movements. When she closed her eyes, she started sighing and releasing more energy.

When she opened her eyes, she said, "I heard 'Good girl.' Those are Mom's words. That's what she called me."

She said, "I want to ask my psychiatrist why he left me when I needed him." I said, "Go ahead and ask him," and did another set of eye movements with her. When she opened her eyes, she said, "He told me 'Lauren, someday we will understand it all.' I know those weren't my words. Oh, my God, those were from my psychiatrist who died in the middle of when I was seeing him and I really needed him."

Life Changes from the Repair & Reattachment Grief Therapy

Lauren's disturbing memories reduced dramatically during the Repair & Reattachment Grief Therapy. The memory, "My mom didn't like men" had been a 10 plus, plus, plus at the beginning of the session. During the session, Lauren said, "It's zero because it doesn't matter anymore."

The memory of Grandma's husband, Lester's, funeral started as a 10 plus, plus, plus. During the connection, she said, "It's almost a 1.5. It's neutral, Rochelle. I was grieving for Grandma, Lester, my father, and everyone who died in my family." Lauren hadn't been aware of whom and what she had been grieving for, but once she was aware of it, the grief dissipated.

The memory that her mom never liked her dad's family started out at a disturbance level of 10. During the connection, she said, "Oh, that's gone way down. It's down past a seven or six."

Explanation of
Bilateral Stimulation

In a Repair & Reattachment Grief Therapy, the psychotherapist provides one or more of the forms of bilateral stimulation to the experiencer while she focuses on a person she knows who has passed away. Bilateral stimulation alternately stimulates the left and right sides of the body, resulting in alternating stimulation of the left and right sides of the brain. The stimulation can be alternating taps on either side of the body, sounds alternating in the ears through headphones, eye movements sweeping back and forth, left and right, and other forms of stimulation of one side of the body, then the other.

It seems that receiving bilateral stimulation while the person is thinking of the disturbing thought or image disrupts the thought and memory pattern so the person reprocesses the thoughts and accompanying images. After a period of bilateral stimulation, negative emotions from traumatic thoughts and images diminish in intensity, often replaced by more rational thoughts and images. Bilateral stimulation is used to alleviate anxiety, fears, nightmares, dysfunctional life patterns, psychological maladies, and post-traumatic stress disorder (traumas associated with combat and sexual, physical, or emotional abuse).

No one is quite sure what happens to the mind and brain during the bilateral stimulation. The activity seems to reorient the left and right hemispheres of the brain so that incidents, images, and thoughts are viewed differently. This change can be seen in SPECT (single photon emission computed tomography) scans of the brain done before and after treatment with bilateral stimulation.

Some have noted the similarity to eye movement in REM (rapid eye movement) sleep in which the eyes move rapidly while the person is sleeping. Dreams occur during REM sleep, so some suggest the bilateral stimulation simulates dreaming, which results in new perspectives and discoveries.

Bilateral stimulation is not related to hypnosis. The phenomena and effects are entirely different. Hypnosis slows the mind and opens the person to suggestion from the hypnotist. Bilateral stimulation speeds up the mind, and the experiencer focuses on inner, personal perspectives and realizations that unfold independent of the psychotherapist.

Forms of Bilateral Stimulation in Use

The action of stimulating the brain bilaterally can occur using a variety of methods, such as eye movements, tapping on the left and right sides of the body alternately, vibrations alternating between objects held in the left and right hands, and listening to audio that alternates in volume levels between the left and right ears.

Eye Movement Desensitization and Reprocessing (EMDR)[4]

The most well-known method of bilateral stimulation is called eye movement desensitization and reprocessing (EMDR). In EMDR, the psychotherapist has clients move their eyes back and forth from left to right following the psychotherapist's hand, a wand, or a light on a light bar. That results in bilateral stimulation because of the eyes' movements left and right.

The psychotherapist helps the person isolate a disturbing thought, image, or feeling to focus on. The psychotherapist sits in front of the experiencer and sweeps his hand, often with two fingers extended, left and right before the experiencer. The experiencer follows the psychotherapist's fingers with his eyes, without moving his head. During the eye movements, the experiencer focuses on the target thought, image, bodily sensation, or feeling.

The experiencer then closes his eyes to "go inside." When he opens his eyes, he describes what he experienced to the psychotherapist. The psychotherapist then repeats the procedure. After a period of time, the process helps reduce the negative effects of disturbing memories.

Other Forms of Eye Movement Bilateral Stimulation

Other forms of eye movement bilateral stimulation are being used today: Rapid-Eye Technology (RET)[5], Eye Movement Integration Therapy (EMIT), [6] Eye Movement Therapy,[7] and Neuro-Linguistic Programming Eye Movement (NLP).[8]

David Grand's BioLateral™ Audio[9]

David Grand is a Licensed Clinical Social Worker with a Ph.D. from International University who has been trained in the use of EMDR. He has developed a series of CDs containing audio that provides bilateral stimulation by alternating the volumes of sounds sent to the right and left headphone earpieces. He has named the audio "BioLateral™ sound." The audio includes ocean waves, music, rain, taps, and other sounds. The Repair & Reattachment Grief Therapy procedure uses his BioLateral™ recordings.

Laurel Parnell's *Tapping In*[10]

Laurel Parnell, Ph.D., a clinical psychologist, is one of the world's leading experts on EMDR. She has trained thousands in EMDR in international workshops. In her book, *Tapping In*, she explains how people can use bilateral stimulation themselves to relieve emotional distress, aid in physical healing, and relax the body. She also explains how it can be used to enhance spiritual practices. The bilateral stimulation comes from a person's tapping himself or herself alternately on the left and right knees or other parts of the body.

TheraTapper™ Hand Vibrations[11]

Another form of bilateral stimulation applies vibrations alternating between the left and right hands using a device called a TheraTapper™. It has a control unit that sends alternating vibrations through cables to two pods the person holds in the left and right hands. The stimulation is like the vibration of a cell phone or pager. It stimulates the left and right sides of the brain through the sensations on the hands.

Traumas in Bilateral Stimulation

Because bilateral stimulation breaks down the habituated barriers the person has against remembering trauma, defenses that have been in place for decades to keep the person safe from remembering abuse or trauma are disrupted. Breaking down the barriers and defenses forces the person to reprocess previously suppressed memories. The experiencer sees the memories as the person now removed from the traumatic incident in time so she can reexamine them from a more objective perspective. In the case of childhood traumas, the experiencer sees the traumas as an adult, not as the younger person who experienced the trauma or abuse.

As a result, the bilateral stimulation methods are very powerful. They force the person to face the memory or trauma without the habituated defenses that had kept it subdued. When the person's defenses are reduced by the bilateral stimulations, he or she may re-experience the suppressed trauma for the first time in years or decades. That is why it can be important for the psychotherapist to be trained in treating trauma that surfaces during bilateral stimulation sessions.

Bilateral Stimulation in Perceived Connections

In the 1990s, some unusual occurrences began in the offices of psychotherapists using this method.

Dr. Parnell's Clients Experience Perceived Connections

Laurel Parnell, Ph.D., is a well-known expert in the use of EMDR (eye movement desensitization and reprocessing) for bilateral stimulation. Dr. Parnell wrote about a client she called Momi, who was terrified of flying because her best friend, Claudine, had been killed in a plane crash in 1974. Dr. Parnell went through the normal eye-movement bilateral stimulation procedure to help Momi reprocess her irrational feelings about flying. After one set of eye movements, Momi closed her eyes and when she opened them, she said that she heard the deceased Claudine speaking to her, saying,

> It's only awful fighting it—that was terrifying. The actual BANG was not awful. And after that it was slightly disorienting—as a spirit—but the worst part of the whole thing was those fearful minutes fighting what was so. What was so awful was confusion and unknowingness. We all were terrified, and we were screaming. We all were very afraid and that was hell.[12]

Dr. Parnell accepted the fact that Claudine was speaking from the other side. She wrote, "There's something about what she said. The other side was fine. . . . Claudine, who's on the other side, is coming over from the other side . . ."[13]

The message had profound effects on Momi's view of life, death, and flying. That was Dr. Parnell's goal for the session, so she didn't explore the connection further. In her psychotherapy practice using eye-movement bilateral stimulation, she doesn't intentionally encourage such connections.

The Repair & Reattachment Grief Therapy Procedure

This chapter expands on the brief explanation of the Repair & Reattachment Grief Therapy Procedure presented in the earlier chapter titled "Believe! We Are Always with You." You will see some of the text from that chapter. We wanted a short explanation in that earlier chapter so you could understand the case studies that followed it. You'll see more detail here.

In preparation for the Repair & Reattachment Grief Therapy, the psychotherapist has the person put on headphones to listen to a recording of barely audible background music and sounds alternating in volume between the left and right ears. That stimulation of the right and left hearing centers provides audio bilateral stimulation. Experiencers wear the headsets during the entire Repair & Reattachment Grief Therapy session, from the time they sit down in my office until the session ends.

I use David Grand's BioLateral™ audio CDs. His Web site is http://www.biolateral.com. I usually use *The Inner Mirror*, Selection 5. However, any of the BioLateral™ CDs by David Grand that include sounds of rain, waves, and music are suitable.

The procedure begins by having the experiencer talk about the deceased loved one for as long as an hour or more. Especially important are the images and memories associated with the person's death. The psychotherapist takes notes about the memories, numbering them to keep track of them. After the experiencer finishes telling the story, the psychotherapist asks the experiencer to rate the memories to indicate how sad, disturbing, or activated each memory is for the experiencer. The scale is 0 to 10, with 10 being the most disturbing and 0 being none or neutral.

The psychotherapist writes the ratings next to the memories in the notes.

After all the memories are rated, the psychotherapist notes which have the highest disturbance. If more than one memory is rated with the highest number, the psychotherapist asks the experiencer which has the strongest disturbance. The highest-rated memory or the memory the experiencer chooses from among the highest-rated memories becomes the target memory for the first part of the Repair & Reattachment Grief Therapy procedure.

The psychotherapist tells the experiencer to focus on that disturbing memory and guides the experiencer through a short series of rhythmic eye-movements to the left and right to provide the visual bilateral stimulation. Then the psychotherapist says, "Close your eyes, go inside, and when you're ready, open your eyes." The experiencer closes her eyes, thinking the words and focusing on the distressing image or thought. She has an experience, usually for a few seconds, but occasionally for ten minutes or more. The experience could be anything: another memory, unusual scene, feeling of sadness, words heard, bodily sensations, swirls of light, sense of a presence, or any other experience. When she is ready, the experiencer opens her eyes and describes briefly to the psychotherapist what she experienced.

In the early sets of eye movements, the images and feelings are associated with the distressing memory the experiencer is focusing on. The person could experience an elaboration of the memory, seeing details about what took place, or could see colors, lights, swirls, landscapes, or other impressions signaling that a perceived connection could be coming. The actual connection usually comes later in the procedure, after the psychotherapist has repeated this procedure several times. However, for some people, the connection happens as soon as the processing begins. And after the first session, most experiencers have the connection more easily, so in later one-hour sessions, the connection can begin as early as the first set of eye movements.

After the experiencer describes what she experienced while her eyes were closed, the psychotherapist has her focus on that experience, regardless of what it was, and repeats the eye movements. There is no discussion or evaluation of what the experiencer describes. The psychotherapist does not guide the experiencer or suggest any direction for the next experience. The psychotherapist simply accepts whatever the experiencer describes, without comment or judgment.

If the memory seems to have lost its impact on the experiencer, that usually means it has diminished or has been replaced by a positive image. The psychotherapist uses the 0 to 10 rating scale to find out how diminished the disturbance for the memory has become. If it has reduced considerably, the psychotherapist goes on to another disturbing memory and repeats the process. In many cases, one memory can unravel the whole connection.

That process occurs repeatedly for the entire Repair & Reattachment Grief Therapy procedure. Usually during the procedure, the experiencers have perceived connections with their loved ones.

The session continues for as long as the person on the other side is available to communicate. That could mean it continues for up to two or three hours or longer. The example in this book in which Emma had a connection with her grandmother lasted six hours.

After the Repair & Reattachment Grief Therapy, there is little debriefing or analysis. The perceived connection contains all of the insights and revelations the experiencer needs to understand the counsel from the loved ones involved in the connection and reorient their perceptions and lives. The healing occurs during the connection. The psychotherapist reads back to the client what came across from the other side and gives the client a copy.

What They Experience with Their Eyes Closed

In my experience, nearly all of the people who come for Repair & Reattachment Grief Therapy will have connection in some form.

It may be of any nature: visual, auditory, tactile, olfactory, emotional, or cognitive.

The experiencer may have a sense of the presence of the deceased, see the deceased, hear the deceased's voice, smell characteristic smells, and feel hugs or kisses. In their most dramatic forms, experiencers can perceive the deceased standing in front of them or have extended conversations with them. They may see the deceased dancing or doing some other activity that was characteristic of them.

If the experiencer has a traumatic image connected to the deceased's death, most often it is transformed into a loving, happy, or neutral one. "I can't even bring up the old memory," they often say.

If the person has disturbing emotions, such as strong guilt or anger, the emotions may need to be addressed first. Usually, they dissipate so the connection can unfold.

More than one person may come through. In one instance, a father came through, had a short discussion with the experiencer, then left abruptly, to the dismay of the experiencer. But within a few seconds, her deceased mother came through to comfort her and explain why her father had left. With that understanding and the joy at having both her mother and father come through, the session ended happily.

Pets that were important to the experiencer may appear in the perceived connection.

Anything may happen. We must expect the unexpected.

Effects on Sadness, Grief, Trauma, and Life Changes

Repair & Reattachment Grief Therapy connections are positive, so the effects on the experiencer are positive. The connection with the deceased heals grief and changes the experiencer's life, sometimes immediately or in the next days. It always changes for the better; they look at the world in a different way. A deep healing has occurred, changing the landscape of their belief system because of the connection.

After the Repair & Reattachment Grief Therapy experience, grief is normally diminished greatly or resolved. They feel a new understanding and direction for their lives. They know without a doubt that their loved one is happy and safe, and that they will eventually be reunited.

Effect of Beliefs on the Connections

Beliefs play no role in the Repair & Reattachment Grief Therapy. The experiencer may be a Christian, Hindu, Buddhist, Muslim, agnostic, or atheist. It doesn't matter what the psychotherapist or the experiencer believe. The outcome will be the same.

For Psychotherapists

You must realize these truths about the Repair & Reattachment Grief Therapy.

The Experience is a Sacred Event

Those in the experience come out of love to change the lives of their loved ones on the earth plane by reassuring them they are alive and well, and that the experiencers should live their lives in joy and confidence in their eternal natures, looking forward to the reunion that is in their futures.

They come to change lives. We are passive observers of a communion between loved ones that is as deep and profound as any connection between human beings can be. In the first millennium BCE and first century CE, the High Priest of the Jewish temples was the only person on Earth permitted once a year on Yom Kippur to walk behind a veil into the inner sanctuary of the Temple, called the kodesh kodashim, sanctum sanctorum, or holy of holies, to have an encounter with God. That was the most sacred event of the year.

Today, every time an experiencer makes a connection with deceased loved ones, he has entered a comparable sacred space normally inaccessible to human beings. There, he communes with loved ones. Psychotherapists who are at this meeting witness one of the most profound events occurring in the modern world. Just as the veil covering the kodesh kodashim is parted to allow an encounter with God, the veil between the other side and this life opens, and people commune with their loved ones in heartfelt gestures of love and caring. Each connection we witness is a sacred event.

The procedure is unlike conventional psychotherapy, so it requires a psychotherapist unlike a conventional psychotherapist.

You must be compassionate, patient, caring, sensitive, loving and have the heart, disposition, and skills. It helps if you are also intuitive and spiritual. If you are normally goal driven, impatient, uninvolved, and distant from your clients, or if you are looking for a new psychotherapy method to book more clients and make money, or if you are interested in the uniqueness of the connections solely for research rather than as life-changing events, we advise that you not attempt to help someone experience a Repair & Reattachment Grief Therapy connection. It is a profoundly personal experience that requires a psychotherapist who cares more for the person than for the procedure.

Time pressures and meeting schedules must not have an influence on you or the experiencer. The procedure must occur in a calm, relaxed, unhurried atmosphere. The timing is not yours. You must be prepared to be led by the experience, not to lead it. That means you cannot schedule the sessions for a 50-minute hour, or even two hours, with a scheduled time to end. The session must continue until the loved ones involved in the connection give it closure, not you and not the experiencer. The sessions normally take five or more hours in a one-day session.

You yourself must be in a good place mentally and spiritually before the session. Be rested. Meditate if you commonly do so. Perform slow-paced, calming activities that morning. Schedule nothing for the afternoon that you must anticipate with anxiety or be concerned about. Be peaceful, unstressed, and focused on the miracle that is about to occur.

Something good will happen during a session. We can't predict what it will be, but we know that something good will happen. At a minimum, the experiencers' sadness will be greatly reduced, and traumatic images will not have such a firm grip on them. But it is very likely they will experience life-changing connections with their deceased loved ones.

Those on the other side are in charge. Neither we nor the experiencer can do anything to influence what happens. We help the experiencer enter a condition of mind that sets the stage for the perceived connection, but the deceased initiate and orchestrate the event. We can only learn what happened afterward when the experiencers describe it to us. We can help the experiencer frame questions and encourage continued dialogue with the deceased, but the answers and the content of the dialogue are beyond our influence.

The loved ones and the energies that make their communication possible know what the experiencer needs better than we could ever know. We must step aside and allow them to take the experience where they will.

The Importance of Following the Protocol

The procedure is simple, but does require following the protocol perfectly. Missing a single step or using a part of the protocol ineffectively will reduce or eliminate the possibility of the person's having a Repair & Reattachment Grief Therapy experience.

Trying to blend this procedure with other methods that you're already comfortable with reduces the likelihood of connections. It is important to follow this Repair & Reattachment Grief Therapy protocol exactly the way it is presented.

You Must Have No Expectations

You need to monitor your own beliefs and enthusiasm as a psychotherapist. Perceived connections are naturally occurring experiences that happen to people when they are in an open, receptive mode, without expectations or straining. If you have expectations that are communicated to the experiencer, that will interfere with their receptive mode. Any expectations on your part or on the part of the experiencer will block the experience. The experience is like a soap bubble floating by. If you reach for it to draw it closer or to move it in one direction or another, it will pop.

The Keys—Openness and Receptivity

The perceived connections occur naturally, on their own. Those who come through are in charge. As a result, your role is simply to help the experiencers come to an open, receptive condition in which they can receive the connection that comes from the deceased. You must not lead or suggest anything about what happens. For example, if the experiencer said "I saw a white light, but nothing else," don't suggest something about a white light from your knowledge or spiritual tradition. Have the experiencer go back to the image of the white light and focus on it; let those on the other side take over helping the experiencer understand the white light.

If the experiencer says, "I want to know if my husband still cares about me" or "I want to ask him whether he can tell me what to do about our grown son," simply say, "We have to see what happens. We are not in control." You and the experiencer must be completely open to anything that might happen.

Reducing the Sadness

The bilateral stimulation does a remarkable job of reducing the experiencer's sadness. That is why you are able to tell the experiencer to stay with the sadness and feel its full intensity. The bilateral stimulation will reduce whatever level of sadness the person experiences.

Most of the perceived connections occur after the sadness has started to diminish. It seems that the sadness, guilt, or grief is actually one of the obstacles to connections. Reducing it allows the love and compassion that created the sadness to emerge, and the connection is the outcome.

As a result, 90% of what you will be doing is reducing the experiencer's sadness. When the experiencer tells you the sadness is diminishing, you can reasonably expect a connection to follow.

We strongly discourage doing Repair & Reattachment Grief Therapy with experiencers whose loved ones have died within the past year. The feelings of grief, anger, guilt, sadness, and all the other emotions that accompany grieving after a death are obstacles to the openness and receptivity necessary for the perceived connection to unfold.

To Learn About the Training

To learn more about the training and whether you are a candidate for helping people experience Repair & Reattachment Grief Therapy, contact us at http://www.rochellewright.com or http://www.RepairAndReattachment.com.

Conclusion

We want to do anything we can to provide access to this wonderful gift to humankind. We will participate in whatever ways we can to help people have the Repair & Reattachment Grief Therapy experience and to train licensed psychotherapists.

Monitor our Web sites at http://rochellewright.com and http://www.RepairAndReattachment.com for new developments in Repair & Reattachment Grief Therapy.

Endnotes

[1] *The Efficacy of EMDR*. (nd). EMDR Institute, Inc. Retrieved from http://www.emdr.com/efficacy.htm

[2] Shapiro, F. (1997). *EMDR: The Breakthrough Therapy for Overcoming Anxiety, Stress, and Trauma*. Basic Books.

[3] Hogan, R.C. (2008). *Your Eternal Self*. Greater Reality Publications.

[4] Shapiro, F. and Forrest, M.S. (2004). *EMDR: The Breakthrough "Eye Movement" Therapy for Overcoming Anxiety, Stress, and Trauma*. Basic Books.

[5] Johnson, R. (1996). *Reclaim Your Light*. Raintreepress.

[6] Beaulieu, D. (2003). *Eye Movement Integration Therapy: The Comprehensive Clinical Guide*. Crown House.

[7] Veselak, C. (nd). *Workshop in Eye Movement Therapy*. Denver School of Hypnotherapy.

[8] O'Connor, J. and Seymour, J. (1990). *Introducing Neuro-Linguistic Programming*. Mandala [Harper-Collins].

[9] Grand, D. (nd). *Biolateral*. http://www.biolateral.com/

[10] Parnell, L. (2008) *Tapping In*. Sounds True, Inc.

[11] The TheraTapper™. (nd). Retrieved from http://www.dnmsinstitute.com/theratapper.html

[12] Parnell, L. (1998). *Transforming Trauma: EMDR: The Revolutionary New Therapy for Freeing the Mind, Clearing the Body, and Opening the Heart*. New York: W.W. Norton & Company, p. 248.

[13] Parnell, L. (1998). p. 248.

Made in the USA
San Bernardino, CA
06 September 2017